"...experiment upon my words..."

D. JAMES CANNON

Published by
DESERET BOOK COMPANY
Salt Lake City, Utah
1970

SBN No. 87747-412-5
Library of Congress Catalog Card
No. 72-148055

To loved ones
who have joined me in this
exciting experiment.

Introduction

This book is the result of a year-long experiment I recently undertook to see if I could apply the words of God, our Heavenly Father, to my day-by-day relations with my fellowmen: my family, friends, business associates, acquaintances, tradespeople, strangers, to everyone I met in my daily life. I also applied the words of God to nature, to situations and conditions, and to activities. In other words, to anyone and anything that entailed a response from me.

I had been disturbed, as every thinking person has, that modern living moves at such a hectic pace that most of us feel considerable stress and have gotten into habits of insulation from others, with a consequent dehumanization of our society.

I have been active in business and industry, in state and local government. I have been a Mormon missionary and bishop, and have never known a time when I was not engaged in church work. And yet I found myself worried and concerned about my need for greater direction and purpose in life and an increased sensitivity to my fellowmen. After much prayerful thought I came to the conclusion that God has given us answers to every problem and is willing to give us additional guidance if we ask him. We need never be alone or confused.

As a result, this idea — Experiment Upon My Words — came to me. I would try for a year, fifty-two weeks, to put to practice some of the words of God in my daily life.

This book is a record of my year, my "experiment" upon God's words. Herein are latter-day scriptural statements. It has been my intent to examine their validity and put them to the test of meaning and significance. The essay that follows each scriptural reference is only exploratory. It is an expression of the author's thoughts after one week of effort to understand and practice the message of a particular scripture.

Because this book is based upon the scriptures and their application in our lives, it is my hope that the reader, in turn, will become similarly involved, invest himself in this reading exercise, and become a participant in the experiment.

My personal experience in taking one scripture per week and putting it to the test, living by it, and applying it to my problems, decisions, and attitudes of daily pursuits has been most rewarding. The principles of the gospel really do work—they are the answer.

I suggest the book become a periodic reading project instead of being read at one sitting. An excellent way is a Sunday afternoon reading and then a thoughtful consideration of its application to your life during the coming week. It's a real spiritual experience. I'm reminded of a statement in Alma 5:14 that applies: ". . . have ye spiritually been born of God? Have ye received his image in your countenances? Have ye experienced this mighty change in your hearts?"

In that spirit I invite you to *experiment upon the words of God. . . .*

Contents

Thankfulness

And he who receiveth all things
with thankfulness
shall be made glorious;
and the things of this earth
shall be added unto him,
even an hundred fold,
yea, more.

—D&C 78:19

1 THANKFULNESS

For a week I tried to receive all things with thankfulness, and it was a marvelous experience.

The things that had irritated me before, such as dull company or bad weather, became not only bearable but actually a pleasure. The difference was in me. And it wasn't a case of fooling myself: it was in taking the opportunity to see people with new eyes, listening to them, seeking to understand them even though they weren't scintillating personalities.

When it was overcast or rainy, I turned to something else, such as reading, writing, or meditating. I found that I even liked adverse weather, because my grateful heart made me realize that it has its own beauty and is a vital part of the cycle of life.

In a short time I began to understand why a person who has been terribly ill and has recovered, or who has convalesced after suffering an injury, is so sensitive to life. When a person has had an escape from death, life becomes precious.

When one receives life with thankfulness, life becomes full of meaning and excitement. It is sensitivity training in the finest meaning of the phrase.

The reward is in the increased awareness that blessing-counting brings.

But the Lord has promised much more. As we grow in appreciation, the things of the earth are given to us. We suspect that when God sees that we have learned to truly appreciate all that he has bestowed upon us, he is willing to grant us access to "the things of this earth." When we have placed proper value upon the spiritual, we are in a position to be grateful for temporal blessings. This was another discovery of that memorable week of receiving all things with thankfulness.

There are other bonuses from living with a gracious and appreciative heart. It increases and enhances the self-respect of other people. I learned that when I develop a real understanding for the feelings and needs of others, *they* have greater self-esteem, they feel better, they respond affirmatively to life. Thankfulness is contagious.

During my week, I developed an awareness of what was happening around me. I began to understand what John Ruskin meant when he said: "The ennobling difference between one man and another is that one feels more than the other."

Life became mine. I became a participant and not a suffering victim. I became the captain of my fate because life was now glorious and meaningful. I became grateful for all that God has done.

". . . in everything give thanks; Waiting patiently on the Lord. . . ." (D&C 98:1-2.)

Declaration of Rights

We claim the privilege
of worshiping Almighty God
according to the dictates
of our own conscience,
and allow all men the same privilege,
let them worship how, where,
or what they may.

—11TH ARTICLE OF FAITH OF THE CHURCH OF JESUS CHRIST OF LATTER-DAY SAINTS

There is probably no surer evidence of a great soul than he who refrains from imposing his particular beliefs and forms of worship on others. Too many people think that what is good for them is also good for men everywhere, that others *must* perform "our" way. Much of the strife and trouble in the world is caused by this kind of invasion.

Even those who have received personal witness that their way of life is right must be wary of demanding others to follow, or regarding them with suspicion if they do not readily accept "our" way of life.

During a week of intensive observation, I saw that some people think that tolerance of an idea implies acceptance of that idea. Therefore, they cling to a restricted set of beliefs because they fear that if they open their minds they will lose what they have found to be comfortable. Nothing could be further from the truth. The gospel of Jesus Christ is not a fragile thing. It cannot be blown away by other winds of doctrine and belief.

We worship Almighty God. Others may choose to worship objects and ideals that are far from God.

We must not abridge their rights. We expect that they will not violate our rights.

If an idea is sound, it will live. If our way is the right way, it will ultimately prevail. It will do no good to dictate and impose. Man responds when he comprehends something that is just and true and is presented to him in love and respect, along with an acceptance of his divine right to freely choose.

A person cannot know the whole truth if he has put on blinders and circumscribed his limited vision of right. He cannot be completely fixed and maintain any willingness to explore. The latter-day religion states unequivocally: "We believe all that God has revealed, all that he does now reveal, and we believe that he will yet reveal many great and important things. . . ." (Article of Faith 9.) This statement implies a spirit of receptivity and intelligence.

A person who desires to truly worship Almighty God must be willing to reexamine his faith. He must remove from his soul the "Phariseeism" that excludes God's spirit. By diligently pursuing right himself and granting this same freedom to others, he worships God in light and truth.

Finally, this Mormon statement about allowing "all men the same privilege . . ." is a solid, meaningful Declaration of Rights—both civil and religious. Mormons believe that they may worship without interference. They freely acknowledge the rights of others to do the same. They hope other men will not interfere with sincere religious practice and thought.

Joy

. . . men are,

that they might have joy.

—2 NEPHI 2:25

3 JOY

"Men are, that they might have joy." This is an idea that ought to dominate our lives. In the face of all the pessimism and hate in the world today, we ought to remind ourselves that God put us on earth to have a joyful experience — not foolishness and frivolity, but real happiness.

Like so many other great words, joy isn't an easy word to define. One thing we know: if we doggedly pursue it, we'll probably never find it. But if we count our blessings daily (and hourly), if we look for the good in people and things, and if we try to do our duty well, we'll probably have joy. In other words, ". . . fill the measure of your creation and have joy therein."

The implication of this scripture is that man is meant to have joy. Once a person truly believes this, he is more likely to look upon life in a positive way. He sees that the people who contribute to the enrichment of life are they who regard it as a great adventure. They are radiant; they have developed a talent for happiness.

During the week of "experiment," I remembered a statement in Proverbs 17:22 about "a merry heart," which indicates that outlook and attitude are important. No matter how well we live by the book, no matter how thoroughly we obey the rules, if we don't have a merry heart we can't have joy. One gets a lift of spirit just by thinking about a merry heart. Even though some people seem basically to be dour, and even though many are beset by bleak problems, everyone can feel better if he tries to look at life brightly for a little while.

I made this personal discovery: when I overcome obstacles, when I learn to choose the right, when I prove myself faithful to God, I realize joy.

In Job 38:7 we learn that in pre-earth life "all the sons of God shouted for joy." There is great value in contemplating why we are on earth. We are not here to hate, to be jealous, to covet, to think dark thoughts and to be miserable. We are here to live purely, to love life deeply, to feel strongly, to act positively. God wants us to be happy. That's our challenge.

Teach

. . . teach one another
the doctrine of the kingdom.
Teach ye diligently and
my grace shall attend you,
that you may be instructed
more perfectly . . .
in all things that pertain
unto the kingdom of God. . . .

—D&C 88:77-78

We are dependent upon each other. I have learned that we have different gifts and abilities. We need to share so that all may be instructed more perfectly, and thus society will be improved. If we need each other, we need to teach each other, and to do it diligently.

This statement implies that we should *communicate* with each other. By doing so, I can profit from your experiences and you can profit by mine. We can learn from each other's thoughts.

For those who say that the "doctrine of the kingdom" only refers to a rather narrow religious dogma, it should be pointed out that the Lord has said that "all things unto me are spiritual, and not at any time have I given unto you a law which was temporal. . . ." (D&C 29:34.) In addition, he says that this is a commandment (D&C 88:77), and he describes many academic pursuits and disciplines, including this qualification: "Of both in heaven and earth . . ." (verse 79).

By teaching one another, every person can start (as one speaker said) "at the shoulder level rather than the ground level." If we hope to start at the shoulder level, if we hope to learn from the ages past and improve on the experiences of others, we must learn to listen as well as teach.

Most of what we call communicating—whether in a discussion circle or sidewalk conversation—is a jousting, with some participants impatiently waiting to interrupt and some who are uneasy about the possibility of being interrupted. It is rare when a person really listens and politely waits to contribute something both germane and significant.

The fact is that questioning and listening are inseparable in all human communication. We improve our minds and learn when we are both receptive to the teachings of others and ready to impart our thoughts and experience to those who can be enriched thereby.

The ultimate objective is, of course, to learn about God: to learn about all things that pertain unto his kingdom, to know what he has in store for us, and to know how we may become like him. John Milton said, "The end of learning is to know God, and out of that knowledge to love him, and to imitate him. . . ." When we teach one another, then, we are drawing closer to God.

A week of intensive effort to apply this scripture in my life proved to me that God's grace *did* come as I tried to be diligent about sharing my knowledge with others. This teaching and learning process is made exciting because of the Lord's promise: "Teach ye diligently and my grace shall attend you."

Accomplishment

. . . for I know
that the Lord giveth no commandments
unto the children of men,
save he shall prepare a way for them
that they may accomplish the thing
which he commandeth them.

—*1 NEPHI 3:7*

5 ACCOMPLISHMENT

We mustn't fear for the exigencies and problems that confront us; we should face life with an affirmative, "God-is-with-me" attitude. Our Father has promised us that he will prepare the path if we will dedicate ourselves to his way. This statement, from 1 Nephi, was made by Nephi to his father, Lehi, after he had assured his father that "I will go and do the things which the Lord hath commanded. . . ."

It has been a zestful challenge to find out that no area of human experience is beyond the expressed concern of the Lord. He has given his commandments —his inspired word—to every problem that may torment man. This is not to say that he has given a panacea for every situation (that is why we believe in prayer), but his revelations through the prophets do shed great light on human needs.

"Experiment" upon the word of God. When a problem faces you, turn to scripture and communication with the Lord. Embark on a program to read God's word daily. Seek to understand the gospel message. Apply it to your life.

When one looks at a problem in the light of day, he knows that God didn't intend that we be fearful and full of doubt. Yet when life is full upon us and we're in the midst of harassment, it's not easy to pause and think that the Lord intends that we face life with courage, strength, kindness, and wisdom. The easy way is to fret and fume, to lose our temper, and to muddle through. Most of us live this way: in quiet desperation.

Most people think that the Lord's way is hard. They resist responding to his commandments. They "murmur" (as Nephi says). We try many things, running hither and yon. But the answer is to renew our lives by accepting God. Once we have made that decision, we have started in the right direction.

I have also discovered that the Lord's "burden" is light and his "yoke is easy." If we really commit ourselves to him and his way, he will prepare our path. This doesn't mean that there is an end to effort nor problem-facing when one accepts Christ. This doesn't mean that we should become slothful because of the easiness of the way. The Lord still expects us to use our resources to the fullest. Our intelligence, our strength, our will are still needed.

But it is inspiring to know that God is with us. It is satisfying to know that we can lean on him: that he is our partner and friend; that he loves us; that we can rely on his guidance and help; that he will prepare a way for us.

Counsel

. . . let thy thoughts be directed
unto the Lord; . . .
Counsel with the Lord in all thy doings,
and he will direct thee for good. . . .

—ALMA 37:36-37

Seven consecutive days of constantly letting my thoughts "be directed unto the Lord" have convinced me that I need to follow this plan all the days of my years.

I've found that when I take a few minutes first thing in the morning to pray to him and then try to keep in touch with him during the day, my life is better, I am more at peace, I have direction, I get things done (probably because problems don't overwhelm me).

I have also observed the truth of this statement: ". . . if any man shall seek to build up himself, and seeketh not my counsel, he shall have no power, and his folly shall be made manifest." (D&C 136:19.)

There is really nothing we do that should be started without counseling with the Lord. He might dissuade us from doing something we shouldn't if we ask his advice—and we might see a problem more clearly if we ask him for help.

When we *counsel with* the Lord, we should not tell or inform; we should *communicate*. We should let him know that we need and want his direction.

If we make a habit of counseling with the Lord, we might even find ourselves being more sensitive to the needs of our fellowmen. When we feel the presence of God, our fellowmen—the children of God—become important to us. We know that they are there, that they matter—to us and to God.

When a person has made this scripture an integral part of his every-day life, he sees a multitude of situations where he needs the Lord. He wonders how he got along before, when he tried to tackle life's problems on his own. He sees now that one man, in concert with God, can face life bravely and with sincere confidence. He has the wonderful assurance that he is placing himself in the hands of Deity, and he knows that God cares.

To seek counsel is to prepare one's mind for the reception of truth. Through counseling with the Lord, our "prejudices . . . give way before the truth." (D&C 109:56.) It is remarkable what happens to the human mind that is filled with pride and self-concern when its owner approaches God for heavenly guidance and direction.

The word "all" (". . . in all thy doings") is significant as one seeks to apply this gospel message to his life. It means that a person ought to confer with the Lord in *every* activity in which he is engaged, and in *every* problem that confronts him.

Commitment

. . . men should be anxiously engaged
in a good cause,
and do many things of their own free will,
and bring to pass much righteousness;
For the power is in them. . . .

—D&C 58:27-28

7 COMMITMENT

Don't wait to do something good until you're forced to do it. Learn not to procrastinate. If something's worth doing, do it now.

It's a common weakness of almost all men to avoid doing something until circumstances or someone in authority forces them to get busy. Most of us enjoy planning if it can be done idly and pleasurably. We don't like the performance of work.

But we have the power to do. We have the power to perform in the way that will be best for us. Our forebears fought for our freedom and we cherish that right, but we seldom use it.

Ours is the power to bless, to encourage, to strengthen, to cheer, to help, to bring to pass much righteousness. If we'll look, we'll see the needs all around us. There is much suffering in our midst, and we can alleviate some of it.

There is a need for people to be involved and to be anxiously engaged. We can bring to pass much righteousness. The power of a motivated person is tremendous, as we can see by looking at people in our own communities who have wrought great change or improvement in institutions.

The halfhearted way is not the kind of engagement that the Lord desires. He knows our works, and he is disturbed if we are "neither cold nor hot." (Rev. 3:15.) He expects us to be anxiously engaged, to be valiant, to be wholehearted about his cause.

He calls us to use our "free will" to create, to build, to improve. After considerable effort in this direction, I get the feeling that the Lord is pleased with human accomplishment. He seems to appreciate his children who make an honest effort. I feel a greater love for him and from him when I show some self-reliance and initiative.

It is a mistake to think that we can isolate ourselves from humanity. What we do or fail to do has impact on society. Our energies are needed to make life better.

So we shouldn't wait until our neighbor's troubles have become our troubles, or ignore a problem just because someone else has it. Quicker than we realize, the sickness, poverty, revolt, crises and pollution may engulf us. The time to act is now, with the free agency and the power that we have.

God will bless our performance.

Truth

And by the power of the Holy Ghost
ye may know the truth of all things.
And whatsoever thing is good
is just and true. . . .

—MORONI 10:5-6

I was led to reexamine the subject of truth when I placed this scripture before me for a week. I was reminded that Pilate asked Jesus, "What is truth?" Countless people have wondered about this. Some people ask the question rather idly, like they toy with a current fad such as "What is obscenity?" But some men ask the what-is-truth question with a sincere yearning to know the answer. Most of us would really like to know the right way.

Perhaps the first step is to learn from the Psalmist: "Remove from me the way of lying . . . I have chosen the way of truth. . . ." (Ps. 119:29-30.) A person has taken a great step forward when he decides that "the way of truth" is for him, and that he will remove falsehood and deceit from his thinking and doing. In his relationships with other persons, he will speak the truth. He will know that truth and sincerity are eternally wedded, so he will seek integrity.

The truth-seeker desires to learn about God and the divine relationship between God and man. He continues in the Lord's way, because he has God's promise that he "shall know the truth, and the truth shall make you free." (John 8:32.)

In my experiment, I began to see that considerable patience was required in the pursuit of truth. I remembered a statement from the Doctrine and Covenants that I "must grow in grace and in the knowledge of truth." (D&C 50:40.) The life of joy is in the man who believes that life is growth, that a person proceeds from imperfection to perfection. Sad is the life of a person who has reached the end of learning and improvement.

The way of truth is to make the Holy Ghost our constant companion. In the process we learn to recognize good. I am learning that I can recognize good by the way it makes me feel. If something comes into my life that makes me feel like a better person, then I know it is good. I am learning that if it is good, it is also true; and I realize that I must make it a part of me or I'll lose it.

No human can adequately convey to another human a full expression of truth. But he can point the way if he is led by the Holy Spirit. In that spirit, I urge every man to commit himself to the cause of truth. It is the only hope in the world. Only when men make a full turn from falsehood and expediency in the direction of truth will we begin to realize peace. "The Spirit of truth is of God. . . ." (D&C 93:26.)

Progress

Whatever principle of intelligence
we attain unto in this life,
it will rise with us in the resurrection.

—*D&C 130:18*

9 PROGRESS

To those who believe that intelligence is something that one is born with and that cannot be enlarged, it may be a bit startling to read the word of the Lord that we "attain" degrees of intelligence in this life through our effort. In recent years, scientists have begun to find that intelligence quotients can actually be increased through brain use. I can assure you—based on personal experience—that a person can improve his intelligence level by study, prayer, and application.

All of our learning should be focused to the goal that Goethe says is "to find out what he has to do," so that our life will have meaning and application. Acquisition of knowledge should not be frivolous; but if it is related to the whole man and to the whole of life, if it is applied and practiced and experienced, it will help man attain to the things of eternity.

I'll sound a warning note, however: one should not seek knowledge and intelligence in order to feel superior. Jesus Christ frequently observed that "the first shall be last," which clearly indicates that one should not be vain and proud in his effort to seek learning.

A sublime aspect of this scripture is that knowledge and intelligence are not for this life only, but are of supreme importance in eternal life. What a tremendous loss there would be if a person's acquired learning were of no value in the life after death! However, we have the Lord's word that all true knowledge will contribute to our eternal progress; literally, "it will rise with us in the resurrection." The prospect clothes the learning process with a special kind of significance and glory.

I've found that the challenging aspect of this scripture is the Lord's reminder that we should keep enriching our minds and get excited about the use of our intellect. God has created mental achievement and intelligence enlargement; so we humans need to give greater emphasis to those things. There is no doubt that a person who improves his mind continually is one who lives a richer life. In addition, his contribution to society can be very significant.

Mortal life is a probationary period. If we seek to attain greater intelligence in this life, we will help to fulfill our probationary purpose here. Without doubt, the same Lord who delighted in telling the parable of the talents will be pleased with our efforts to improve our intelligence. We will progress in this life and earn the right to eternal progress in the life after this.

Endure

. . . press forward

with a steadfastness in Christ,

having a perfect brightness of hope,

and a love of God and of all men.

. . . endure to the end. . . .

Ye shall have eternal life.

—2 NEPHI 31:20

10 ENDURE

It is a regenerating experience to get an insight into possible perfection in Christ. No other system or organization (except the Lord's church) offers that kind of hope. As important as they are, neither a man's work nor his citizenship can lead him to perfection. Without belief and goal in Christ, man flounders in a welter of divergent ideas and philosophies.

I can testify that self value and soul satisfaction come to a person who will "press forward with a steadfastness in Christ."

This is one of those scriptures in which every word and phrase is significant. For instance, I am stimulated by the words "a perfect brightness of hope." It is a memorable phrase: one of those that stays in your mind and crops up at odd moments. I love both its implications and its applications.

Love is mentioned hundreds of times in scripture, but "a love *of God* for all men" is a fresh approach to a traditional belief. What it means to me is that I ought to regard other persons the way God does. I ought to abandon my human tendency to just tolerate their existence and take on a God-like attitude of active concern and interest in their welfare. I cannot take God's place as their father, but I can understand their being part of a heavenly family, and therefore my brothers. Then I can more fully duplicate a *love of God* for them. I serve them with greater understanding.

The trend of society is to jump when things get tough: to change jobs, to move to a new neighborhood, to dissolve a marriage, to run away. It's good to "endure to the end." What this means to me is that if we prayerfully chart a course of action and dedicate our lives to Christ, then we will stick with our course through both the high and low cycles.

One of the troubles of refusing to endure is that we develop a habit of evading and avoiding. Men need constancy in their lives, but they'll never get it if they always move away from trouble and difficulty.

The promise of eternal life is the highest recognition God gives to his children. Psychologists have hailed the importance of every human's developing a distinct sense of self. One university instructor has added that a man should have an "ultimate goal to know who he is, where he is going, what he wants to do with his life."

The highest sense of self comes when a person begins to understand that God loves him, that he is on earth for a purpose, and that God has outlined a plan which, if followed, will bring him fulfillment and perfection.

Righteousness

11 RIGHTEOUSNESS

Several years ago I noticed a sick feeling inside me if I hurt someone else. I also observed the opposite: when I did good, inside I felt warm and whole. Thus, when I saw those words in the Doctrine and Covenants about one's "bowels" being "full of charity," I recognized them as valid.

Plato identified four cardinal virtues: prudence, fortitude, temperance, and justice. To these have been added the Christian virtues of faith, hope, and charity. It is a pleasing experience to try to apply these to our daily life, to let them "garnish" our every thought. The promise in these words is that by letting moral excellence adorn our lives, we will find fulfillment.

Many writers view realism as negativism. They like to tell about the seamy and unpleasant and to ignore the true and beautiful.

Each of us needs to give more thought to virtue and less to its opposites. We need to look upward more often. We need to develop the habit of looking for good rather than evil. When we want to be *realistic,* we must realize that man is basically good, and that life is not viewed accurately if only its dark side is shown.

Although much has been said elsewhere about the Holy Ghost, it is good to remind ourselves that he can be our "constant companion." The Holy Ghost is given to us through priesthood power, but we must continue to cultivate spiritual presence and association. He can be our guardian angel. He can be our comforter and guide. He can help us over difficult spots. He can help us see clearly. He can point the way. Our responsibility is to fully accept him and welcome him into our lives.

We have earthly companions and friends who mean much to us; when we lose one we mourn. In like manner we can have great joy in having a heavenly companion. Even though we may not see him, we can feel his presence and are assured that he will always be there—even through death.

I have also noticed that the Holy Ghost is a marvelous comforter when sadness comes into our lives. When all else seems lost, we can turn to our "constant companion" for comfort and peace.

We do so by seeking righteousness continually and overcoming weakness and sin. Righteousness is virtue in action. It is the application of both the "natural" virtues of Plato and the Christian virtues exemplified by Jesus. It is the lifelong seeking after truth in all things. I've found that it is never tiresome, never boring; always challenging and meaningful. I have found that when I look for the righteous course of action, I always do better.

I recommend righteousness.

Spirit

Behold my Spirit is upon you, . . .
and thou shalt abide in me,
and I in you;
therefore walk with me.

—MOSES 6:34

A young girl who was struggling to express the deep feeling of spirituality in her soul told her listeners that she wished that all of us who strive to impress the world would spend some time working to impress God.

Afterwards, I thought a great deal about the difference between impressing the world and seeking to impress God. To do the latter, a person cultivates God's spirit; he keeps his commandments; he is humble; he yields himself to God's service. Figuratively, he seeks to abide in the Lord. Herein the man has the heavenly promise that if he does this, God will give man his spirit. It is a wonderful thing to abide in the Lord, and feel him abide in you and walk with you.

Once a person has enjoyed the Lord's spirit, he never forgets the experience. He continually hopes for the time when he can once again walk in its light. It is not easy for a human being to abide in the Lord. Weaknesses, temporal activities, and other involvements prevent us from doing this even when we want to.

What we need to do is to set this goal as primary and make it an overriding principle of our lives. When we make this kind of a resolution, all else becomes secondary or nonexistent. Pettiness is pushed into the shadows and finally overcome.

It is really a matter of prayer. We ask God to forgive us of our trespasses. We ask him to love us. We ask him to give us strength and take away our fear. In order to improve our communication with him, we seek to learn more about him.

With God as our ideal, we begin to change our life to meet his standards. Life becomes meaningful, exciting, and enjoyable. And it isn't a prideful or boastful kind of confidence: it's a whole-souled feeling.

If you seek, you'll find.

When a person realizes that "the kingdom of God is within" (Luke 17:21), he cultivates the heavenly spirit, knowing that no problem or obstacle can then deter him. He knows that it is within his power—with the Lord's assistance—to face life bravely and with purpose.

Periodically I need spiritual renewal. So I start every day with a personal prayer to God. I tell him that I would like to "keep in touch" with him during the day. My best days are when I think about God often and when I feel him close to me as I seek to abide in him.

Vigor

Let thy bowels also be full of charity . . . and let virtue garnish thy thoughts unceasingly. . . .The Holy Ghost shall be thy constant companion, and thy scepter an unchanging scepter of righteousness and truth. . . .

—D&C 121:45-46

Cease to be idle;
cease to be unclean;
cease to find fault one with another;
cease to sleep longer than is needful;
. . . that your bodies and your minds
may be invigorated.

—D&C 88:124

13 VIGOR

As our modern life gives us more leisure, there is a greater tendency to fill the hours with idleness: long stretches in front of the television set, or just plain indolence (in the guise of escape from the problems of a complex world). People who do this are those whose main idea of leisure is to kill time. They consider work as a curse, and embrace the idea that one should make as little mental or physical effort as possible.

Increasing industrialization and automation have taken from man the pride of workmanship that he enjoyed when work was individually done. This trend, however, needn't deprive man of one of life's greatest experiences: the deep joy of creativity, the satisfaction of a job well done, the peace of mind and soul from faithfully performing one's tasks.

We have heard it said that "cleanliness is next to Godliness," so it may not be surprising to be reminded that the Lord has said that "no unclean thing can inherit the kingdom of God" (Alma 40:26). A person faced with a choice of being clean in body and mind or being dirty needn't be troubled about which is God's way. The fact is that a person who is unclean generally has a low outlook on life.

If we work diligently and keep ourselves clean, we will not have either the time or inclination to "find fault one with another."

The idle mind (that mind which is not intent upon its own projects) is the one that is critical of others.

On the subject of too much sleep, it can be observed that this may be one of the "little sins," but one that prevents many people from realizing the abundant life. Planning one's life is so important if one wishes to make the best use of his time. The best way is to follow the scriptural admonition: Don't "sleep longer than is needful." Benjamin Franklin observed that "he that rises late must trot all day, and shall scarce overtake his business at night."

One of the major problems of the world is that so many people do so little to improve conditions or make a real contribution to life. Too many lives are frittered away in too much sleep. Every individual should, of course, have enough daily rest. But every individual should determine how *much* is "enough." I would venture to say that a tremendous number of hours are wasted in sleep that is unneeded.

The total effect of abiding by this portion of God's advice is that our bodies and minds are invigorated. It's great to arise in the morning refreshed and ready to face the day — and it's amazing how troubles and problems dissolve when we face it with vigor.

. . . we search the prophets,
and we have many revelations
and the spirit of prophecy;
and having all these witnesses
we obtain a hope,
and our faith becometh unshaken. . . .

—*JACOB* 4:6

When we have all the evidence, why shouldn't we have faith and hope? We have the word of God through the prophets and through revelation, so why not let this fact be our guiding light, so that our lives are directed to good?

There is so much in the world to deflect us from the right course. There is so much that causes us to think and react negatively, and to be without hope. We lose faith in ourselves and in our fellowmen.

But if we think about "all the witnesses" that God has given us, we become positive. We see that it is possible to take the two steps noted here: *to search* and *to acknowledge*. When we earnestly search for the word of God, we are blessed with the spirit of revelation and prophecy. And when we acknowledge these witnesses, we are blessed with hope, followed by a strengthening of our faith.

This is clearly a statement of optimism. It is a reminder to look for all the witnesses, all the evidence of God's love, that are before us.

Hope is literally an enlargement of the soul. Hope

is the forerunner of faith. Hope comes to us as we put forth some effort to find out what God has said through his prophets and what those prophetic messages mean to us. We are quickly rewarded in this search, because the Lord gives us greater spirituality through revelation and prophecy. By thus recognizing the word of God, "we obtain a hope."

As we thus enlarge our soul, we become capable of living by faith. A new and deeper understanding comes to us, and we become more in tune with the Spirit of God. A strengthening of faith is accompanied by a greater spiritual power.

Literally, "our faith becometh unshaken. . . ." This is the kind of faith that I would like to have. To me, it does not imply a closed mind. It means being willing to receive and accept. It means a faith that is firm, that doesn't waver "like a wave of the sea driven with the wind and tossed." (James 1:6.)

The scripture quoted from the Book of Mormon suggests that we should start small and grow big. We need to start hoping, for this is a basis of great faith. And the wonderful aspect of it is that we don't need to be foolishly optimistic. God has reminded us that we have the evidence upon which to base our hope.

I've found that the man who develops his faith gets glimpses of spiritual power, because there are blessed occasions when he commands and there is response. Far from becoming intoxicated with this kind of power, the righteous man praises God and rejoices in heavenly goodness.

Seek

. . . seek ye out of the best books
words of wisdom;
seek learning, even by study
and also by faith.

—D&C 88:118

15 SEEK

To seek diligently is to live beautifully. To seek learning out of the best books is to fill one's hours with happiness, growth, and fulfillment.

To seek learning by faith is the necessary ingredient, however, because obtaining learning from earthly sources is not enough. A little learning is a dangerous thing when it is done without learning by faith. Of course one shouldn't turn away from earthly learning or man's efforts to improve and expand his mentality, but one should also cultivate the ability to communicate with God and to exercise faith in the learning experience.

God's command to read and learn is definite and given without equivocation. Men ignore this statement by the Lord only at the peril of eternal growth and progress, and yet many people almost completely disregard this part of revelation.

I have an acquaintance who freely admits that he never reads a book. "Too busy," he says.

Keeping the nose to the grindstone may be all right, and to fill every day with purposeful and energetic work is fine, but to let the days and years go by without a determined pursuit of added or new learning is to miss the big picture.

A well-known advertising campaign features the headline, "Give Me a Man Who Reads. . . ." The point is that the sponsoring company has discovered that a reading man is more valuable as an employee than a nonreading man.

When all else is said and done, however, the value of reading is the genuine joy it brings to the reader. He is never bored. Time doesn't weigh heavy on him. He doesn't have to depend on someone or something else to entertain him.

To those who need to be commanded by God in order to believe, I should add that this scriptural statement is preceded (verse 77 of Section 88) with the words "I give unto you a commandment." This is why I referred to it earlier as "God's command to read and learn." The advice is: get busy, embark on a mind-improvement program, and start reading good books. It is never too late to learn.

There seems to be a definite lack of identification with a set of guiding principles in the world. We all need an orientation toward God's truth. We can get that direction by seeking wisdom.

Peace

And ye will not have a mind
to injure one another,
but to live peaceably,
and to render to every man
according to that which is his due.

—MOSIAH 4:13

16 PEACE

We take ourselves too seriously. We judge others too harshly. Peace not only doesn't prevail in the world—it doesn't function too well in our day-to-day relationships.

I found out when I lived with the verse in Mosiah for a week that these statements apply to me. I also noticed that others were infected.

In our personal communication—whether in the home, office, or shop — we need more of the light touch. We need to be more relaxed in our dealings with others. We need to develop a sense of humor that is healthy and positive. An accurate observation of our life was made recently by a person who has the light touch: "Talk about tense times—even shaving cream is under pressure."

Each of us seems to need a regular reminder to

"not have a mind to injure one another," and to learn to live in peace. There is so much turmoil, so much strife and aggression, so great an emphasis on militancy and "power," that it is refreshing to learn that God tells us to be peaceful. History has taught me that a human can't "render to every man his due" unless he does it peaceably.

The message of this scripture is one of involvement rather than withdrawal. To learn to live peaceably with others implies increasing one's participation in human affairs, accepting added responsibility, learning to share, asking for mutual respect, learning self-control. It is an active kind of experience to try to understand, to listen, and to become enthusiastic about another person.

For families to learn to live together and be happy is for all members thereof to learn to live peaceably and to learn not to injure one another, either physically, mentally, or emotionally. The greatest art known to man is to live with others harmoniously and helpfully.

I have been surprised to see how much more a person can accomplish if he will adopt a peaceable attitude rather than one of aggression. He does not need to be soft or weak; he can perform his duty and with evident kindness and goodwill.

To give another person his due is to let him know that you respect his humanity and intelligence; you have no intention to find fault or to injure; you desire to live peaceably.

Happiness

. . . consider on
the blessed and happy state
of those that
keep the commandments of God. . . .

—*MOSIAH* 2:41

17 HAPPINESS

If you would be happy, keep the commandments of God. It's as simple as that. To help you make that decision, I'll share a few thoughts that came to me during the days I gave special consideration to this scripture.

First, you have to give priority to being happy. There's no use talking about happiness if you don't believe it is highly important to you. Happiness is one of the things God expects of you.

Next, I found out after much prayer, study, thought, and observation that keeping the commandments of God is absolutely necessary for true happiness. We have to be whole-souled about the gospel. I not only took note of all that I saw and heard during that week; I also thought back about past experiences. I recalled that I *had* never seen a happy person among those who were violating God's laws.

I'm not saying one has to be perfect to be happy. However, "those that keep the commandments of God" are those who are sincerely *trying* to do all that the Lord expects. Those who are apathetic, those who pick and choose from among God's commandments, and those who figure they've done enough and who stop trying are definitely not candidates for a "blessed and happy state."

Third, I found that it is genuinely helpful to consider people who are happy because they are doing God's will. I noticed that they are at peace with themselves: they are not prejudiced: they enjoy life without intoxicants or artificial stimulation; that they are clean and healthy.

Fourth, I saw that keeping the commandments of God had become a way of life with these people, and is therefore neither a drudgery nor a difficulty. I'm impressed that happy people get that way by looking at the bright side of things.

If we believe in God or desire to believe, we accept the idea that he will ultimately win in the struggle of good and evil. We optimistically acknowledge the strong possibility that light will supersede darkness.

That leaves us with the decision about whether to be happy or unhappy. This scripture tells us that we can be happy by responding to God's word. I can testify that it's an honest statement.

Boldness

See that ye are not lifted up unto pride; yea,
see that ye do not boast in your own wisdom,
nor of your much strength.
Use boldness, but not overbearance;
and also
see that ye bridle all your passions,
that ye may be filled with love. . . .

—ALMA 38:11-12

A person needs self-esteem. He needs to feel that he is important and that he counts. But to feel this way, he doesn't need to boast or flex his muscles or be full of self-pride.

The world would have us believe that we've got to make a show of strength or wit or intelligence to attract attention and build our self-image. Many advertisements are geared to the idea that if we use XYZ product, we can improve our appearance or our ability so that we can impress others, and (the implication is) be a happier individual.

God's way is for each individual to be filled with love, not be overbearing, use self-control. His way is a reversal of the world's way, but he has invited us to try it. When we find that strength is found not in outward display of prowess, but in an inward faith and confidence, we see that—as usual—the Lord's way is the right way.

Contrary to a widespread portrayal of Jesus and his followers as weak individuals is this scriptural statement that we should "use boldness." Those two words give us a valuable insight into the nature of God. He invites his children to be confident and purposeful. In the four gospels and the other works that tell of our Savior, we see that he has given a view of an ideal life: humble and full of love, but potent and energetic. He did not withdraw from the world. He loved his fellowmen and to be with them. When it came time to show strength (such as when he cleansed the temple), he had the boldness to do the job. The word "boldness" means having a resolute will; being self-assertive; being a person in whom others can believe. It means being able to take calculated risks with a minimum of anxiety. As Goethe said, "Boldness has genius, power and magic in it."

The individual who is bold has confidence, believes in himself (because there is no reason to distrust himself), figuratively "puts his best foot forward." The key to the right amount of boldness is found in the first three lines of our scripture: avoiding pride, not boasting in our wisdom, and not boasting in our strength.

Finally, we are advised to "bridle" our passions and "be filled with love." Numerous thoughtful people have suggested other words for controlling passions—words such as "bend," subdue," "restrain," "moderate," "govern"—but they all imply the same idea. The important point is to not allow our passions to run rampant, for if they do we can hardly be filled with the spirit of love.

God has given us some sound advice. If we follow it, we can become more like him. This scriptural statement points us in that direction.

Love of God

. . . every thing which inviteth and enticeth
to do good, and to love God,
and to serve him,
is inspired of God.

—*MORONI 7:13*

19 LOVE OF GOD

Here is a guide and an excellent "rule of thumb" to anyone who is trying to decide whether he should do one thing or another. If one course helps the individual to draw closer to God, and the alternative takes him further away, then the first course is the one to follow.

Just try it for a week, starting with decisions about how to spend the Sabbath day. Jesus said that the Sabbath was made for man, and not man for the Sabbath. It is not enough to say that hair-splitting rules should be laid down about the Sabbath day—that is too much like the Pharisees in Jesus' time. It seems right that each person ask himself if a given activity on the Sabbath day is conducive to the Spirit of God.

Two thoughts suggest themselves in discussing this matter: (1) no man should set himself up as judge of what another man does or does not do; (2) no man should seek to justify his actions by misusing this scriptural quotation. It is easy for a person to say to himself, for instance, that a sports activity is all right for the Sabbath day because it is doing him good. That kind of rationalizing seems to stretch the meaning of the scripture.

At the same time, we agree that humans should not try to pass judgment. Once again, the responsibility falls on the shoulders of each individual. This means that we will be a lot closer to making a right decision if we seek the Lord in prayer and then prayerfully, honestly, seek to weigh all the facts and consider the alternatives.

We can know which direction to go by evaluating three criteria: (1) Does it help us to do good? (2) Does it help us to love God? (3) Does it help us to serve God? That action which helps us in one way will probably help us in the other two ways, and thus we will know that it is "inspired of God."

Many good-seeking people grope in the dark because they lack direction. Most people genuinely desire to do good. Most parents are desirous that their children do the right thing. Most people really would like to help their neighbors. Most citizens would like to think that their community is better because of what they've done.

All of us need more heavenly guidance. We generally don't like to have someone spell out for us the exact steps to take, but we do appreciate some guidelines. We love our freedom, and we will generally choose the right when we see clearly.

This scriptural statement encourages rational thought and prayer and yet leaves the final decision up to us. It is of real help if a person will put it to use.

Scripture

And whatsoever they shall speak
when moved upon by the Holy Ghost
shall be scripture, and
shall be the will of the Lord,
shall be the mind of the Lord,
shall be the word of the Lord,
shall be the voice of the Lord,
and the power of God unto salvation.

—*D&C 68:4*

Communication with God is not dead. He is close to us not only when we pray to him, but he can also be heard through those who are moved upon by the Holy Ghost. We hear the Lord's will, mind, word, and voice expressed by the person who speaks when he is so moved. In addition, we feel the evidence of God's power in such an experience.

It is easy, however, for some men to wrongfully adjudge inspiration from God. It is easy for a man to be swayed by his own wishes and think that the Lord has given him direction. This is why the Lord has made clear that both the listener and the speaker should be led by the Spirit of truth, and "he that preacheth and he that receiveth, understand one another, and both are edified and rejoice together." (D&C 50:22.)

People who attempt to communicate with the Lord, therefore, need to really be in tune with heaven. They need to be completely receptive to God's direction. They cannot be negative, critical, or hateful. They need to cleanse themselves, purify themselves, and humble themselves.

When the one who speaks is led by the Holy

Ghost and he who listens is "in touch" with the Lord, the results are marvelously spiritual and edifying. A person can have this experience in the physical presence of someone who is led by the Holy Ghost or he may have it as he reads the messages of prophets who were similarly moved. There are countless experiences of people who, as they have read scripture, have enjoyed the great impact of the Spirit of God.

If we are not favored with God's direct manifestations, we can hear his voice and know his word by listening to and reading from the prophets. In this way we can feel the presence and power of God through spiritual communication.

I noticed another implication as I gave special attention to this scripture. I began to understand that the listener must curb a tendency to be critical and envious of the speaker. He must be filled with love and friendliness. He must look beyond the speaker's faults. In essence, he must be receptive to God's Spirit.

It is also a wonderful blessing to know that God has so honored us that humble man can speak for the Lord. It is an opportunity for *every* man, not just a chosen few. Every husband and father is king, prophet, and revelator in his own home. He can invite the Spirit of God into that home. In a similar way, no one is beyond the Lord's concern. Every person can enjoy the dignity of God's love and interest.

It's a wonderful experience to learn to respond to the Spirit of God.

Health

And all saints who remember to keep
and do these sayings,
walking in obedience to the commandments,
shall receive health . . .
and shall find wisdom . . .
And shall run and not be weary,
and shall walk and not faint.
And I, the Lord, give unto them a promise. . . .

—*D&C* 89:18-21

What a promise!

This is the last part of the Word of Wisdom. It testifies that *all* who honor the spirit and letter of God's word found in this section of the Doctrine and Covenants will be directly blessed by God.

The appellation "saints" is not restricted to a few holy people; it refers to all who would like to follow Christ. In a real sense it is "adapted to the capacity of the weak," so all can benefit by God's advice.

This message is reminiscent of the statements of First Corinthians (3:16-17) and Alma (7:21), in which our bodies are likened unto temples of God. We are advised that "filthiness or anything which is unclean" cannot "be received into the kingdom of God." We are reminded, therefore, that we must not "defile the temple of God," which temple we are.

In all of these statements it is clear that it is not

only wise to observe principles of health and cleanliness—it is absolutely necessary, if we intend to return to God's presence.

Our bodies are precious. In the Pearl of Great Price we read that "in the image of his own body, male and female, created he them, and blessed them. . . ." (Moses 6:7.) We can thus see that man is the culminating creation of God, made in his image. Therefore, he is displeased if we violate that creation.

The Word of Wisdom tells us not to take deleterious substances into our body. It suggests moderation in the consumption of certain substances. It extols the value of "every herb . . . and every fruit."

It is interesting that these health rules, considered to be rather strange when given in 1833, are being found by medical science in the twentieth century to be accurate.

It is important, of course, that we continue our efforts to actually prohibit those things which deaden and injure (such as drugs). It is equally important that we redouble our efforts to educate people on the harmfulness of other substances that also injure and defile.

In addition to the obedience value of response to God's word, there is definite value and joy in having a clean, undefiled body. The Lord has not promised us freedom from injury or death, but he has promised us direct results from our faithful response to his Word of Wisdom.

Prepare

. . . this life is the time
for men to prepare to meet God;
yea, behold
the day of this life is the day
for men to perform their labors.

—ALMA 34:32

Our life is a probationary period. We are here to prove ourselves—whether we will be able to return to God or whether we are not worthy of that honor. In this brief span of mortality, we are supposed to educate ourselves, learn self-control, love our fellowmen, and build our spiritual lives. Then the Lord will know that we have filled the measure of our creation, and we are ready to take the next steps in eternal progress.

Thus, in this life we prepare to meet God. We perform our labors, whatever they may be, with diligence and loyalty. We realize that every day is valuable, because in it lie the eternal verities. How we respond to its challenges and opportunities is a microcosm of our eternal life.

My personal study of this gospel message indicates that there is no implication that we must always be involved and busy. An important part of preparing to meet God is to learn to appreciate his handiwork, whether it be the beauties of nature or the nobility of the human creation. Jesus Christ himself was mildly critical of Martha when she was "cumbered with much serving," as contrasted with her sister Mary, who took the time to enjoy the presence of Jesus. Learning to appreciate life and to be happy in it are important parts of living. One should not miss the glories of this world. This is God's creation, and I imagine he appreciates those who take time to admire what he's done.

One of the challenges of life is to learn that many things, while important, are not to be overdone. It is to be committed, but not fanatical. It is to seek learning and wisdom, but not pride. It is to work, but not become a slave to one's work. It is to love others, but keep one's individuality.

My interpretation of the scripture is that it suggests a dynamic, problem-solving kind of preparation. It recognizes a problem, collects pertinent facts, reviews the data, thinks of alternatives and new combinations, and recognizes a possible solution. Finally, it tests the solution (by performance of one's "labors") for accuracy and applicability.

The preparation-performance idea of this scripture has been tested and proven effective. I recommend it to you. I know that when I unthinkingly wade into my work, I generally fail to achieve the goal, or I ultimately get there after much more effort and worry than needed. But when I have taken the steps noted above, I have a much better possibility of success.

Change means continuity, progressive evolution. To prepare to meet God is that kind of evolution—constantly learning to do better.

No power or influence
can or ought to be maintained
by virtue of the priesthood,
only by persuasion, . . .
by gentleness and meekness,
and by love unfeigned.

—*D&C* 121:41

23 GENTLENESS

So much of what we do is by the play of power. It is refreshing, therefore, to be reminded that God never intended that we get things done by force. Whether it be manifest in religious authoritarianism, corporate strength, militancy, or any other means of possible oppression, God's way is the way of peace, kindness, and "love unfeigned."

This is what life is all about: to give a helping hand to someone in need. We shouldn't go through life pushing others around. And yet, a great many people either do this or are part of organizations that are guilty of coercion and domination.

No person and no organization has been truly successful in exercising naked power. For a time, many may attain some success in a program of repression, but in the long run, the oppressed either fight back successfully or the dominating organization falls apart.

In the case of God's priesthood, he does not want it to become domineering. He asks that bearers of that priesthood use kindness and regard instead of ruthless power. He knows that his children can be saved only by peaceful persuasion in a good cause. He believes so strongly in free agency that he has made this a guiding principle in the plan of salvation. Anything that abridges or circumvents free agency is not of God.

It is an easy thing to impose one's will on one's fellowmen. Jesus pointed this out when he told the parable of the ungrateful servant. We have seen it happen dozens of times in religious and secular history. We are made aware of it almost every time we pick up the newspaper. In our most introspective moments we become aware of how oppressive we ourselves can become.

This scriptural admonition reminds us that we can and should do two things: (1) eliminate unwarranted use of power in our activities and thoughts, and (2) oppose oppression and coercion wherever and whenever we see it. In other words, we can learn to hate misuse of power and can learn to love our fellowmen.

A warning note, however: we who oppose the misuse of power must be careful not to fall into the same pattern of oppression and coercion. The best way is to cultivate gentleness and goodwill in all of our dealings. It is pleasantly surprising to see how often people who have been using force turn the other way when they see that gentleness works.

When you let another person know that you love him "unfeigned," it is amazing how you and he can work together.

First Estate

And we will prove them herewith,
to see if they do all things
whatsoever the Lord their God
shall command them;
And they who keep their first estate
shall be added upon. . . .

—*ABRAHAM* 3:25-26

24 FIRST ESTATE

Our first estate is our life here on this earth, which is where we will be proved. If we "keep" it faithfully, the Lord will see that we are "added upon."

This scripture suggests to me why we are here on earth. It further reminds me that God is watching us to see if we keep his commandments.

During the week of experiment on this scriptural statement, I was led to think about the gift of life, the wonder and beauty of it. I can say yes to the question in Alma 5:14: "Have ye experienced this mighty change in your hearts?"

Keeping my first estate has been a process of adopting the long-range view as well as learning "line upon line, precept upon precept. . . ." (D&C 98:12.)

Just as we *keep* a plant by watering it, we *keep* our first estate by improving upon it. For example, we learn to withstand the temptation to sin, and we learn not to take for granted God's enlightenment.

Today we see a lot of pessimism in the world. There are some who are trying to overthrow substantial elements of society because they feel we are not moving in the right direction.

My musings, however, convince me that we have failed in two ways: (1) to conduct our lives honorably and demand that government do the same, and (2) to adequately tell our story to youth and to the downtrodden. In other words, we haven't run things as well as we could have done; we have shown a definite tendency to gloss over our mistakes, and we have allowed a "communications gap" to develop.

We need to be less defensive about our failings. We should be willing to look at them afresh. If there are mistakes, let's seek to correct them.

I think this is all part of keeping our first estate. The Lord has frequently said that he doesn't like complacency and apathy in his children. He obviously would like us to be more responsible. Ours is a role of stewardship for both the physical earth and the needs of humanity.

The way to make improvements is to draw closer to God, for he has told man over the centuries that he will not countenance prejudice and hate. He has told us what to do to be "added upon" both in this life and the next.

Wisdom

And see that all these things are done
in wisdom and order;
for it is not requisite
that a man
should run faster than he has strength. . . .

—*MOSIAH 4:27*

God's will is that we do all things "in wisdom and order." He apparently is desirous that his children learn to do their duty wisely and in an order, and not frantically. He is obviously pleased when we perform with excellence, but seems disappointed when we are erratic and weak. He has said that he doesn't like the trumpet that gives an uncertain sound. On the other hand, he is saying in this scripture that he is not pleased with the person who rushes breathlessly through life.

During my week of concentration on this scripture, I gave a lot of thought to how I could be a willing, responsive worker, and yet not "run faster" than I'm able. There is a fine line between *anxiously engaged* and overdoing.

I believe the answer lies in planning my work. I remember a meaningful statement in the Doctrine and Covenants: "Organize yourselves: prepare every needful thing. . . ." (D&C 88:119.) I always do better when I plan, but I get more done and do it more efficiently if I prepare for the work.

In most projects there is always much to be done, so there's a real temptation for a willing person to work hard. Unfortunately, however, there are some who do not work and who accept no responsibility.

God recognizes man's limitations. He has not only inspired this prophetic statement, but he has also made it clear that he will "prepare the way" when he asks man to do something. In Doctrine and Covenants 10:4, he has revealed another guideline to the "do not run faster" concept: ". . . or labor more." This gives additional support to the idea that he is genuinely interested and concerned.

I am convinced that we could conduct our business more efficiently by doing things in "wisdom and order." One trouble is that we approach too many tasks with a half-hearted attitude. This is true of most group effort; the potential of the individual members is rarely fully used.

As a member of a few committees and a participant in several projects, I have found God's advice in Mosiah 4:27 to be particularly helpful. I commend all of King Benjamin's speech (Mosiah 2 through 4) as a further enlightenment to all who would serve their fellowmen.

Study

. . . you must study it out in your mind;
then you must ask me if it be right,
and if it is right
I will cause that your bosom
shall burn within you;
therefore, you shall feel that it is right.

—*D&C 9:8*

Two thoughts are brought to mind as one reads this scripture: (1) this is the way that inspiration from God works when one is performing a project in which he needs the Lord's guidance and approbation; (2) this is an excellent procedure to follow in any work of creativity.

Don't let anyone be misled about heavenly inspiration. It does not come with a snap of the fingers. It does not come by simply wishing that God would respond. It comes when the Lord knows that we are putting forth a strong effort to do our part and are in need of his help. Great things can be done when a firm partnership between God and man is established. God will give liberally, but he needs to be earnestly sought by the person who realizes that he lacks wisdom and needs God's help.

The idea of "humble dependence upon God and manly reliance in self"* is a principle we should all incorporate in our lives. Both the westward movement of the Mormon people and their subsequent colonization program were planned by a leader—

**Author unknown.*

Brigham Young—who leaned heavily upon both man's knowledge and God's inspiration.

Any given project is nearly always better when it has been presented to and reviewed by someone else. Whether it is a written piece, an activity project, or a plan of organization, it needs another viewpoint. It is always helpful to seek God's assistance. He has promised that a feeling of rightness will burn in the bosom of the person who asks, and that "a stupor of thought" will attend the person whose work is not acceptable to him.

Even the very suggestion of studying it out is worthwhile. I have found that when I remember to devote earnest thought—the power of my whole mind — to a subject, I accomplish much more.

Many people limit their appeals to heaven to those matters with which they think God is concerned. To my knowledge, God has never limited his interest to ecclesiastical matters. I have felt that I could approach him on any matter. Even though this particular message was given to one individual in response to his need, I have felt that it has meaning and relevance to all people.

The scripture is evidence that God's light is throughout the world and that many men have responded by creating suitable items of study. If we would comprehend the things of God, we should seek to understand these things through study and then ask God for help. If we do, he will clearly confirm and bless.

Search

. . . ye should search diligently
in the light of Christ
that ye may know good from evil;
and if ye will lay hold upon every good thing,
and condemn it not,
ye certainly will be a child of Christ.

—MORONI 7:19

27 SEARCH

In a time when "truth is relative," and there is a rather widespread belief in "situation ethics," it's good to be reminded that it is possible for man to know good from evil. It is both refreshing and encouraging to know that the Maker has said that if we will earnestly seek good and not condemn it, we may become like him: "a child of Christ."

The pendulum has swung from persecution and prejudice to the far opposite side, sort of a "nothing is bad" attitude. We have seen that intolerance has been very harmful in our society, but we have allowed a new kind of intolerance to dominate our lives as we have dismissed the idea of any absolutes, any final truth.

Unfortunately, the ones on the far left are so militant, so demanding, that those on the far right are moving against them into what might be a dreadful confrontation. Among the silent majority in the middle, there are too many who are apathetic, and too few who believe that truth, beauty, and goodness are obtainable, who abhor intolerance and hate, and who love life and their fellowmen.

More recruits are needed who want to be guided by the light of Christ into living affirmatively. They are the ones who desire to "lay hold upon every good thing."

There are enough good men in the world that they can overcome evil by truth *if they try.*

The danger is that we may allow our communities to be turned into armed camps. The fearful thing is that we may sit on our hands while immorality, viciousness, and destruction run rampant.

A week of study on this principle has suggested to me a strong need for people to know the difference between good and evil. We are bombarded with so much news that we tend to take a neutral position on everything. We seem to be living in a day of non-involvement. Perhaps we need to spend more time evaluating particular issues and less time inhaling so much. In other words, we need to follow the Lord's advice to "search diligently in the light of Christ."

The Lord has directed his charge to each individual to take those steps necessary to become a disciple of God. When others see us doing good or seeking good, they will be encouraged to do the same. When they see us standing for right, they will stand with us. I know this to be true because I have tried it. By such effort we may become once more a credit to our Heavenly Father.

Be Prepared

. . . if ye are prepared
ye shall not fear.

—D&C 38:30

We see it over and over again. We see it under all circumstances. The person who is prepared delivers the goods. He makes his presentation or displays his completed work with pride and dignity—and without fear.

Probably unknowingly he has fulfilled God's promise that fear will disappear if a person prepares. It is a heavenly injunction of great portent. It can be applied in almost every situation in life.

It is especially apparent as a person faces death. If he has prepared himself he can face death without fear. That is, if he has lived honorably, has sought God in prayer and thought, has tried to faithfully serve his fellowmen. If, on the other hand, his life has been spent in wasteful, meaningless pursuits, he will not be prepared to meet his Maker. That is the inexorableness of life: we suffer the consequences of our behavior.

I remember a funeral where the deceased and the closest mourners had procrastinated their time of repentance and preparation. It was far more mournful than the normal funeral, because onlookers could feel the fear and concern that racked the family.

During my week of concentration upon this subject I could not find anything that was more pervasive and dominant than fear. In nearly all cases our fears are completely unwarranted. Whether they are or not, however, God's advice is that all we need to do is to adequately prepare. When we do we will find either that our fears are unfounded or that we have the strength and wisdom to meet them unflinchingly.

If we do not prepare we worry and fret, we run from life, we retreat before an imagined enemy, we lose hope and faith in the purpose of life. Probably the most damaging effect of fear is the loss of direction we suffer. Attendant to it is the urge to find a scapegoat—a cause of our difficulty. Our sense of values has been knocked askew by our fears, so we often blame others who do not deserve our attack.

We need more people who have confidence in the essential goodness of man. I would like to be worthy of Goethe's charge to "be ashamed to die until you have won some victory for humanity." I hope to be counted among those who have replaced fear with faith.

Prepare yourself with prayer. Prepare yourself by honest work. Prepare yourself in wholehearted service. Spend your energy in preparation and you will find that you have none to expend on fear. The Lord has promised it. I have witnessed enough evidence that I know this scriptural statement is true.

We believe in being honest, true,
chaste, benevolent, virtuous,
and in doing good to all men. . . .
If there is anything virtuous, lovely,
or of good report or praiseworthy,
we seek after these things.

—ARTICLE OF FAITH 13

29 VIRTUE

If there is anything our world needs right now, it is for men to dedicate themselves to doing good. We have had too much of malcontents who do evil at every opportunity. Most men are sick unto death of filth all around us, riots, violence. But these same men do little or nothing about the problem, other than grumble.

What is sorely needed is for good people to make a commitment, not to fight violence with violence, but to consciously do good. We need people to make an unequivocal stand for an expression of high values. If we don't do that soon, there will be a backlash. There will be a physical battle (or many of them), as law-and-order citizens fight for their rights against those who would destroy.

We have allowed the libertarians to label good people as prudes and do-gooders. They have used sarcasm and cynicism so potently that we have retreated into silence and let the militants take over. It is no wonder that our youth are mightily confused. Most of them cherish goodness because they've had glimpses of how it works. But they dislike the inaction of the older generation at a time when our way of life is being threatened.

The thirteenth Article of Faith—inspired of God—is a rallying cry for virtue. It is a divinely motivated statement of man's decision to look for the good in people rather than the bad. It is an action statement, not just an abstract thought. The emphasis is on the *doing* and *seeking after.* One cannot be benevolent in a vacuum: he must express that feeling in the midst of men and their problems.

It is a personal creed: in the face of obscenity, I will be chaste; even though some men are dishonest and devious, I will be honest and true; even though the daily news and gossip seem to specialize in unpleasantness and conflict, I will seek that which is of good report and praiseworthy. Anyone who believes in virtue must be actively engaged in guaranteeing equal rights to all men.

The time is now to be aggressive and bold in the cause of right. We need to believe so strongly in freedom that we will firmly oppose oppression and discrimination, and make sure that the rights of men are not trampled upon.

We will speak with a clear voice to those who produce magazines and movies that we have had enough of filth and degradation. We will give our support to the Rule of Law and the democratic process.

We will speak up for virtue and be silent no more.

Receptive

. . . open your ears
that ye may hear,
and your hearts
that ye may understand,
and your minds
that the mysteries of God
may be unfolded to your view.

—MOSIAH 2:9

One of the most recurring pleas of God to man is that he be open-minded, receptive, ready to be instructed. I have observed that the people to whom Jesus directed his opprobrium were those whose minds were closed.

Is it any wonder that a prophet has said ". . . if ye can do no more than desire to believe," the word of God will begin to grow within you? This is what the Lord asks—that we open ourselves to his word. For this purpose he has blessed us with ears, hearts, and minds. If we will let his truth come into us, he will bless us with untold wisdom and direction. It's a marvelous promise.

We may conclude that since the light of Christ has been given to every person, we should cultivate this same receptivity to the teachings of great men. We should reflectively examine what they have to say. We should encourage others to do the same. Perhaps we can counter the human tendency to look at others' ideas with prejudice and misunderstanding. There is a great need in the world for tolerance of ideas.

I am impressed with the value of cultivating the

"scientific mind," that is, assembling as many facts as possible on any matter and studying them rationally before taking action. If we wish to follow God's advice, we will add to this approach love and charity toward our fellowmen. We would do well to seek the guidance of the Lord—to cultivate the prayerful spirit. This is all part of being receptive.

What we may learn when we open our ears, hearts, and minds may be criticism of something we've done or failed to do. When we encourage a receptive attitude, we invite both praise and censure. My experience arising from this scriptural injunction is that any possible criticism is worth the open mnd. I've also learned that the receptive person must be prepared to receive praise and place it in its proper perspective. This is just as important as receiving criticism.

In either instance it is important to learn to be objective, rational, and understanding. At such a time it is well to remember the biblical advice that we "put on the whole armour of God that [we] may be able to stand against the wiles of the devil." (Eph. 6:11.)

We should be receptive to the things of God, but withstand the evils of the adversary. Even with that attitude, every person is confronted with much wickedness. It is wise, therefore, to be receptive and seek to extract all that is good from the world around us. Our challenge is to not let evil overwhelm us or alter our relationship with God.

Reason

And now come,
saith the Lord, . . .
let us reason together,
that ye may understand.

—*D&C 50:10*

31 REASON

It made me feel good that God would "reason" with me, but I was puzzled as to how we could do it. After all, I'm mortal and down here, and he's immortal and up there. Besides that, I'm nothing and he's everything.

I confess it took me a lot longer than a week to come to a satisfactory answer. When I started conjecturing and didn't obtain an answer, I began to believe that this scripture only applied to a select few. Finally, after much study and prayer, I came to a realization (and it seems obvious now) that God loves us so much that he desires to be in close communication with us.

I firmly believe that God is willing to manifest himself unto man. A statement in the book of John (14:23) indicates that: "If a man love me, he will keep my words: and my Father will love him, and we will come unto him, and make our abode with him."

If I believe God is omnipotent, I must believe that he can do anything he wishes to do—including face-to-face communication with man.

However, in spite of everything, our Heavenly Father will not contravene the principle of free agency. The responsibility is on us to initiate the asking. It is beyond my understanding as to how he hears my petition, but I know that I can talk with him directly in prayer, and that—even though he hasn't made a physical appearance to me—I can get the help and direction I need. His response to my petition may not be exactly what I had hoped for, nor is it the same that another man might give me if I were to reason with him. But what I receive from God is always much greater and better than my request!

It is always thrilling to me to learn anew of my relationship with God. No earthly or human recognition is so satisfying to my human yearning for acceptance. It's a good feeling, of course, to have the praise of men, but I've found that it is temporary and meaningless compared to divine approbation.

If we want to talk with a great man, we usually have to go through intermediaries, but we can talk directly with God. There's no question that he listens to us and responds.

Another aspect of reasoning with the Lord is worthy of attention: the books of prophetic statements. Think about it for a moment—much of what man has done is either not recorded or the records have been lost or garbled. But we can get a rather clear picture of the God-man relationship by studying scripture. This experience is a kind of reasoning activity. The result of our reading scripture is that our understanding is enlarged and strengthened.

Charity

Why do ye adorn yourselves
with that which hath no life,
and yet suffer the hungry,
and the needy, and the naked,
and the sick and the afflicted
to pass by you, and notice them not?

—MORMON 8:39

One man—no matter how wealthy he is—can expect to alleviate much suffering with acts of charity. I have observed this as I have visited several areas of the world. I do not feel that a person need be ill at ease if he has acquired some wealth. *But*, if a person ignores the needs of his fellowmen and expends his means completely and selfishly for his own adornment, mankind suffers, and the Lord is grieved. This is what I have learned from experimenting with the foregoing scriptural statement.

The lessons of history, and especially religious history, are clear: men are blessed in temporal ways when they remember God and try to do his will. But too often men turn from God to material things and notice not their fellowmen, except those who can help them gain greater wealth.

A particular instance of the goodness of the Lord is in Malachi 4:8-10, where the Lord promises that when a person tithes he will "pour out a blessing, that there shall not be room enough to receive it." One might say, therefore, that a person who has learned to live with wealth and is still generous and helpful to the needy is a person who lives close to God. Our challenge is to keep materialism from standing in the way of spirituality. We should be humble and teachable because it is right to be that way, not because we are forced to be so.

People who need help are close at hand—we needn't look far. We can give relief to some of them in a direct way and to some through organizations. We don't need to be wealthy in order to do good. If we have no material resources in sufficient abundance, we can give of ourselves: we can give service.

Jesus said: "Lay not up for yourselves treasures upon earth. . . . lay up for yourselves treasures in heaven. . . . For where your treasure is, there will your heart be also." (Matt. 6:19-21.) Place your faith and regard in people instead of things. Don't let them "pass by you, and notice them not."

We cannot ignore the needs of society. A man who works hard and creatively deserves a full and fair reward, but we all also owe a debt to society. Through our decisions at the voting booth and our continued attention to government, we have a voice in the community. Therefore, we all share in the guilt of oppression and poverty in our midst.

The second line of the scripture reminds me that too many men are engrossed in spending their means on meaningless things. I certainly believe that part of our public and private funds should be devoted to beauty, but not to baubles. I believe that God is displeased if we invest our time, effort, and money on "that which hath no life."

Talent

. . . Thou shalt not
idle away thy time,
neither shalt thou
bury thy talent
that it may not be known.

—*D&C 60:13*

Two words that are prominent in this scripture are *time* and *talent.* My first thought is that there is a "talent" in being a good citizen in one's community. The citizen who buries his capability w h e n it is needed is doing his society a disservice. For example, there are times when a citizen should *speak out* on a matter of crucial importance. If he remains silent, if he withdraws, he is burying his talent.

I assure you that talent development is fun. Growing in skill perception is great. I've had an awakening in my life whenever I've learned something new, such as playing ukelele or singing harmony, or making my family happier by being a better father.

There is a close relationship between using one's talent and making good use of time. Obviously, God has seen this and united the two ideas in this scripture. It is important to remind ourselves constantly that we only have one life to live, and how we spend our time and talent will pretty well determine how we will ultimately be judged by God. He has made it very clear that time is precious, and that he has given us a rather liberal portion of time to accomplish good and learn to overcome evil.

We abdicate our responsibility to humanity as we selfishly seek what we think is personal satisfaction. One thoughtful writer has noted that ten wasted minutes each day will add up to a work week and a half in the course of a year. It is quite easy to idle away our time, so every person should carefully analyze his habits and activities.

Seneca observed that men will go to battle over a slight loss of property, but they give no thought to a rather large loss of time. Men will oftentimes engage in meaningless pursuits and not realize that they are giving away that which is most important and irreplaceable.

Two key words in the dictionary describe talent—"natural endowment." God has given man some great natural endowments. It is his expectation, I'm sure, that we joyfully, purposefully use them.

The underlying (and unexpressed) message of this scripture to me is that God is urging us to make good use of both time and talent. This life is so important that we must realize that there is a close limit to our probationary period. None of us has a long lease on life. None of us can safely smother our capabilities and talents.

I am a better person for having been reminded that my time and talent are both valuable and needed. I hope to use them to make life better.

. . . faith is not to have
a perfect knowledge of things;
therefore if ye have faith
ye hope for things that are not seen,
which are true.

—*ALMA* 32:21

So we don't have a perfect knowledge. We still believe our spiritual "intuition" tells us that something is true. Or it may guide us away from something that is evil. It would be impossible to put our feelings into words. It is difficult to fully express them to someone else.

As I studied this scripture I remembered that Christ had used some strong language to urge his followers not to cast their "pearls before swine." Jesus was thus warning his disciples not to talk about spiritual matters with those who were not receptive. He was also saying, I believe, that we should be careful about trying to define an extremely personal matter for others.

You see, even though faith is not a mass movement, it is nevertheless essential to a spiritual and happy life. He who asks in faith shall receive knowledge and answers to all of his righteous needs. ". . . without faith you can do nothing; therefore ask in faith." (D&C 8:10.) It is required for the establishment of God's work. Miracles are wrought by faith. One receives the Lord's law by faith. Faith is needed to endure to the end. Parents teach their children by faith. We overcome evil by faith. People are healed by faith. It can accurately be said that nothing great is ever accomplished without faith.

Now, I'd like to share with you how I analyzed faith. A start is made when a person is willing to receive, to consider. Next, he must humble himself; I've learned that no one who is haughty and proud can learn faith. He must keep the commandments of God. He must keep in communication with him. Faith doesn't come by signs. It doesn't come by boasting. It will never come by sin or shortcuts, nor when one breaks the law. It will come by responsiveness and goodness. It will come when a person seeks earnestly to know God's truth. It is a gift from God.

A significant key to the subject is found in the final two lines of this scripture. ". . . hope for things that are not seen, which are true." These words bring to mind a statement made by Emerson: "All I have seen teaches me to trust the Creator for all that I have not seen." Trust ranks high as an essential part of faith.

In addition, I have found that faith is by no means blind belief or obedience. It requires a combination of intellect, purification of heart, a spirit of inquiry, a genuine "desire to believe," and a trusting spirit. Since its use has launched all significant enterprises, I recommend the practice of faith to everyone who is trying to improve life.

Free

I, the Lord God, make you free,
therefore ye are free indeed;
and the law also maketh you free.

—D&C 98:8

35 FREE

The times require that we address ourselves to the subject of freedom. It is essential to peace in the world, but I feel that freedom is grossly misunderstood and misapplied.

Sadly enough, many among us mistake freedom for license. One of the problems of today is that too many assume that freedom is to have the liberty to do as one pleases without being subject to any law. On the other hand, some who profess a love of freedom construe that it is a violation of that principle to live differently than the believer. He suspects the person who has a different appearance, who may have different political beliefs, or whose value system is different.

Perhaps both the lawless libertarian and the do-as-I-do citizen are misinterpreting freedom. A truly free man believes in the Rule of Law ("the law also maketh you free") and realizes that there is some restraint to impulses and passions. He understands that the principle of freedom does not grant any man the right to do just as he pleases. Free agency is basic to both God and man. Wise men before us have seen that the law honors the plan of God. There is one law for all men, all men are equal before it, and no man can be punished except for the violation of that law.

It is well known that freedom for some men has been denied or withheld. There is still discrimination before the law. We must eliminate this impediment to freedom. We must make sure that all men are free and equal. And we must not wait to be forced by militancy and riot to assure that freedom for all men. God has decreed it, and many wise men have confirmed the fact that law makes us free.

Consider this statement: "We believe that no government can exist in peace, except such laws are framed and held inviolate as will secure to each individual the free exercise of conscience, the right and control of property, and the protection of life." (D&C 134:2.) The fact is that "governments were instituted of God for the benefit of man; and that he holds men accountable for their acts in relation to them, . . . for the good and safety of society." (Verse 1.)

In another place (verse 4) in this "Declaration of Belief regarding Governments and Laws," we are told that "the civil magistrate should restrain crime, but never control conscience; should punish guilt, but never suppress the freedom of the soul."

Freedom is of God. He lives by it. He expects men to live by it. To fulfill our divine missions, we must devote ourselves to the principle of freedom for all men.

Choice

. . . And they are free
to choose liberty and eternal life . . .
or to choose captivity and death. . . .

—2 NEPHI 2:27

36 CHOICE

In order for a man to pattern his life after God and have joy in the process, he must have free agency. With this kind of freedom it is possible that a man may "choose captivity and death. . . ." But a person is worth little unless he has that freedom of choice.

A week of thought on this scriptural quotation has given me the encouragement to look at the subject of freedom of choice on a continuing basis. I have become intrigued with the subject and have therefore been attracted to a statement by Arnold Toynbee: "My own view of history is that human beings do have a genuine freedom to make choices. Our destiny is not predetermined for us; we determine it for ourselves. If we crash, it will be because we have chosen death and evil when we were free to choose life and good."

The essence of choice is knowing and understanding both sides of a question. In addition, to enjoy freedom of choice brings the obligation to be responsible. When a person takes the road to captivity and death, he chooses license instead of liberty. He believes that he can do as he pleases without restraint. He believes that if his view is contrary to law and order, he may engage in civil disobedience.

In most cases, a person does not consciously choose "captivity and death," but he chooses a way of life that takes him in that direction. On the other side is the person who knows that the essence of freedom is self-control and that eternal life is predicated upon honoring the individual, i.e., a recognition that the greatest glory of God is his creation of man.

As with Adam, man proves himself when he has free agency. The Lord says: ". . . I have set before you life and death, blessing and cursing. . . ." (Deut. 30:19.) He urges us to choose life, "That thou mayest love the Lord thy God, and that thou mayest obey his voice, and that thou mayest cleave unto him: for he is thy life, and the length of thy days. . . ." (Verse 20.)

When one realizes that every day—perhaps every hour—his choices and decisions point him toward life or toward death, he begins to comprehend the importance of praying and preparing and performing in the Lord's service.

Well-doing

. . . be not weary in well-doing,
for ye are laying the foundation
of a great work.
And out of small things
proceedeth that which is great.

—D&C 64:33

37 WELL-DOING

The foundation of a great work is laid when people love to do their jobs well. I'm impressed with the idea that a community—or any cooperative undertaking—becomes successful when the members produce efficiently and creatively. The same is true of a man's individual enterprise, whether it be an invention or a home do-it-yourself project. The man whose joy comes from careful workmanship is the one who does something great.

At the moment I can't think of one truly great project or program that didn't start small. It is true that there are spectacular success stories all around us. Our modern day is marked by amazing growth and change. And there are many who believe that sudden success can be theirs with little or no effort. They dream of that event. However, in most cases, even the so-called sudden success is preceded by strong application of practice and preparation. People who receive ready acceptance have generally had a small success (or perhaps several) before the world has recognized them. Those "small things" may even have been some projects that were disappointments or failures. And an unseen factor is the blessing the Lord gives the dedicated individual.

To avoid becoming "weary in well-doing," a person must have not only powerful motivation but also intense persistence and endurance. He must be strongly goal-oriented. When his wife complained that he was a visionary man, Lehi (who was not weary in well-doing) said: "I know that I am a visionary man; for if I had not seen the things of God in a vision I should not have known the goodness of God, but had tarried at Jerusalem, and had perished with my brethren." (1 Nephi 5:4.)

To perform a great work, a person must have the "visionary" quality; he must think and plan big. He must possess considerable innovative ability. Along with this he needs a genuine love of work, because the one without the other produces either an unstable individual or a dull person.

I suppose that many individuals dream of "laying the foundation of a great work." Nearly every person occasionally gets an insight into his potential. It's sad that so few realize the dream. But it's impressive to me that God has pointed the way in this scripture. In effect, he is saying that through every-day endeavor we can lay a "foundation of a great work." If we are willing to put forth our best effort on a persistent and continuing basis, we will ultimately produce something great.

It's a profound statement of faith in human potential.

Gifts of God

. . . deny not the gifts of God,
for they are many;
and they come from the same God.
. . . and they are given
by the manifestations
of the Spirit of God unto men,
to profit them.

—MORONI 10:8

One of the best practices each individual can engage in is to acknowledge the gifts of God. When one counts his blessings, things begin to fall into perspective. He begins to overcome discouragement and self-centeredness. He begins to see that no matter how great his problems, God has been good to him in many ways. The assets far outweigh the liabilities.

A person's thinking goes outward when he contemplates the gifts of God. He can think about the Lord's goodness to him individually and to mankind generally. He probably will be led into a new appreciation for God's handiwork and the beauties of this life.

The lesson to me is that God has given me many gifts. I will count them, cherish them, seek to use them in service, and do my best to improve them.

The accomplishments of man are marvelous: in this technological era we see new inventions and new ways of doing things every day. In each case, if we wish to take advantage of, say, a new labor-saving device, we must pay for the equipment or machine. But we too often take for granted the much greater gift of God because it is there for us to use, misuse, or ignore. His creations are all around us but we do not see them—probably because they have always been there.

The fresh air, the earth beneath us, the flowers and trees, the water, and thousands of other gifts of God are there for us. But if we have thought about them, it is probably only to see how we can use them to our advantage. Instead of being aware and appreciative of these manifestations of God, we have often polluted and despoiled them.

God's gifts are here to "profit" us. That word does not imply exploitation or conquest. It means to benefit us, to make our lives happier and more meaningful. The Lord has made it abundantly clear that man must not exercise unrighteous dominion. The species of animals and plants were not placed here by a loving Father for man to kill in his lust for wealth and power. I believe that God placed them here—along with all else on earth—to help man to learn to manage wisely and honor God's gifts in the process.

What we all need are "the manifestations of the Spirit of God. . . ." By cultivating that spirit, we may come to an awareness of the gifts of God. We may—before it is too late—realize that his gifts are offered to us to use for our edification and then pass them on to succeeding generations to enjoy.

Love

And no one
can assist in this work
except he shall be humble
and full of love,
having faith, hope, and
charity,
being temperate in all things. . . .

—D&C 12:8

39 LOVE

A daily restatement of this scripture has done wonders for me. It has come to mind on occasions when I have needed direction and inspiration, often several times each day. So to you who feel the need for a guide to daily living, there is none better than this one.

What is said here is that we are of no use to the Lord if we are not in tune with him and with our fellowmen. Too many of us in the world live in a dog-eat-dog atmosphere, live by the philosophy of power and advantage, of arrogance, of disregard of God and our fellowmen. It's a great thing to be reminded of the importance of being sensitive to the Lord and our fellow beings here and now.

I'm reminded that I must be full of love, not just tolerant of God and man.

Our Father in heaven has given us six qualifications for being useful: (1) be humble, (2) be full of love, (3) have faith, (4) have hope, (5) be charitable, and (6) be temperate. A person perhaps can't give equal importance to all of them at the same time, but by recalling God's words at any given moment, he can pick out that which is needed as a guide to him at that time.

For example, there are occasions when I need to be reminded to be temperate, so I refrain from overeating, or taking the extra sweet, or staying up too late, or idling too much—any one of a number of ways of being intemperate.

The Lord's advice to be "temperate in all things" supports the idea of moderation and avoiding extremism. It is an adjunct to D&C 89, the "Word of Wisdom." Being temperate also entails the thought that "it is not requisite that a man should run faster than he has strength." (Mosiah 4:24.)

I have observed all kinds of intemperance since memorizing this scripture: not only the intemperance of drink, drugs, and tobacco, but an over-indulgence in eating, sleeping, working, pursuing a hobby, and even doing nothing.

After seeing these, I have made up my mind to seek to be temperate, as the Lord urges. It is good for me and of great value to society.

The implication of this scriptural message to me is that one must truly dedicate and qualify himself for service through living and thinking more completely with our Father and humanity. This is the kind of devotion to duty that the Lord needs and requires.

We are dependent upon each other's well-being. A thinker named Sala said: "God has ordered that men, being in need of each other, should learn to love each other, and bear each other's burdens."

Natural Man

For the natural man
is an enemy to God, . . .
unless he yields to the enticings
of the Holy Spirit,
and putteth off the natural man
and becometh a saint
through the atonement of
Christ the Lord. . . .

—*MOSIAH* 3:19

This is one of those memorable statements that I read several years ago; I remembered particularly the line about "the natural man is an enemy of God. . . ." My memory also retained the words that advise us to *put off* the natural man. When I again found the entire scriptural reference, rememorized most of it, and started to use it intensively for a week, I discovered a reawakening and renewal of spirit.

It is one of the most challenging thoughts in scripture. A week of close reference to it has not been enough. It is one of those statements that comes to mind continually.

Specifically, self-control, as one part of putting off the natural man, should be a joyful experience. It brings many corollary blessings: a person puts himself in communication with God; he becomes more sympathetic with those in need; he finds a special kind of happiness in asceticism; he cleanses his body; he arrives at a greater appreciation of things because he is more sensitive and perceptive.

To the prospective disciple who intended to follow Jesus, the Master stated that the candidate should "deny himself, and take up the cross. . . ." (Mark 8:34.) Unless a person is willing to put off his natural inclinations, Jesus knew that he could not become a worthy follower.

One could expand this idea into all commendable spheres of action. One does not excel or achieve unless he is willing to practice some self-denial and put forth genuine effort. Benjamin Franklin stated it succinctly: "There are no gains without pains."

Not even happiness can be had without subduing the impulses in favor of obedience to the greater good. Self-discipline can help foster inner peace.

All about us we see self-denial depicted as harsh, intolerant, gloomy, unpleasant, priggish, stuffy. Instead, I have learned that to be happy, enthusiastic, progressive, creative, optimistic, one must learn that he can't have everything he wishes. Some things are not for our good, so we should learn not to be self-indulgent.

An interesting insight is obtained when I think of the song "America the Beautiful." One line says: ". . . confirm thy soul in self control. . . ." In other words, strengthen your faith and your spirit by practicing self-discipline. Self-control is a sound way to verify to God and man that you have dedicated your life to truth.

That renewal of spirit which has come to me is that I have come closer to becoming "a saint through the atonement of Christ the Lord."

But learn that he who doeth
the works of righteousness
shall receive his reward,
even peace in this world,
and eternal life in the world to come.

—D&C 59:23

Every person who seeks a code of living should know this divine truth: he who seeks to do what is right shall have a double blessing—peace in this world and eternal life in the world to come. Everywhere people are seeking peace of mind. For many, their search seems to be manifest in escapism, such as a new spouse, freedom from children and work, and a general shrugging-off of responsibility. But the truth is that people find peace of mind in doing "the works of righteousness."

I can testify that a person *does* receive a reward when he performs and serves honestly. Peace comes into my soul whenever I try to do good. Just as surely as it comes to me, I believe wholeheartedly in God's promise of eternal life to all who try.

Peace in this life also means joy in this life. If the Lord wants us to be happy and have peace, then why is there so much misery, captivity, destruction, and bloodshed in the world? Because there are not enough who are seeking righteousness.

Sydney J. Harris tells about a grocer, a deacon in his church, who was heard to call downstairs before breakfast to his clerk: "John, have you watered the rum?" "Yes, sir." "And chicoried the coffee?" "Yes, sir." "And sanded the sugar?" "Yes, sir." "And dusted the pepper?" "Yes, sir." "Then come up to prayer."

The change for the better starts with me. If I can be righteous, others will change. It is remarkable how responsive people are to a good example.

I'm impressed with the suggestion given in Moses 6:59: ". . . enjoy the words of eternal life in this world, and eternal life in the world to come. . . ." It's quite a challenge to ask yourself if you truly *enjoy* God's offerings.

Much of the trouble in the world—both past and present—is due to people's not practicing what they profess to believe. This scriptural statement lays strong stress on the *doing*. There is inspiration in performance: happiness, well-being, a sense of accomplishment, peace of mind and soul. Anyone who will put forth the effort will become the elect of God.

We must learn that our actions must be consistent with our best thought. We believe, so we must put our beliefs into our performance. I have noted that too many times we sit as spectators while the game of life is played by others. Sometimes we get emotionally involved in shouting, but we rarely decide to get into the game.

I am pleased that this scripture encourages me to get more involved in the world. It may seem paradoxical to say it, but greater commitment can also mean more real peace of mind. I urge you to try it and see.

God's Glory

. . . this is my work and my glory—
to bring to pass the immortality
and eternal life of man.

—*MOSES* 1:39

This short scripture has marvelous meaning in two ways: it tells (1) of God's concern for mankind, and (2) of man's importance. If this is truly the Lord's chief concern and occupation, then our human effort becomes significant, especially if it is responsive to God's purposes. Our commitment is to participate with God in his work and glory.

Bringing to pass "the immortality and eternal life of man" is a potent thought. On man's part, it requires devotion, faith, service, endurance, coupled with the grace of God. God's concern is demonstrated in the fact that he gave to all mankind his Son, whose atonement is the supreme grace. He also sent the prophets to help point the way.

The prize of immortality and eternal life is great beyond comprehension. There is not only *hope* beyond the grave, but a blessed assurance that this is the chief concern of God.

The use and placement of words in this scripture mean much to me. For example, many men have extolled the virtues of work, but herein the Lord has made it equal to glory, and has enthroned it as the supreme heavenly function.

As with other scriptures that give dignity and purpose to man's existence, this statement offers to man a strong self-image. If man is important enough that the Lord's major concern is to help him, to work with him, to relate to him, he can see that he has a place in the divine scheme of things.

I have been reminded of this idea both during the week of my special attention to it and in the period that followed when I heard and read so much about the need for a man "to assert his humanity" (as one writer worded it). Here is evidence that man is that important.

When we know that God recognizes man's selfhood, we see that our human society should equally provide for the dignity of all of its members. One young man from Watts, California, said that the main reason for the revolt in his community was to help restore the importance of each individual, including the dignity of the head of the home—the father. We cannot countenance plunder and destruction, of course, but we need to face the thought that our society has probably not adequately provided for the maximum growth of *every* individual.

I have begun to view the handiwork of God in a new way when I have realized that it is there for me. I believe that when men understand this blessed idea, they will not hate and destroy, but they will treasure what God has offered and will desire to preserve God's work so that succeeding generations will also know of his love.

Intelligence

The glory of God
is intelligence,
or, in other words,
light and truth.

—D&C 93:36

43 INTELLIGENCE

The mind can enrich all of life. When its power is directed toward intelligent and rational thought, society benefits. When it is directed toward degradation, humanity suffers. This is probably what God meant when he said that his glory is intelligence. I would imagine that God is disappointed when man uses his mind for darkness and falsehood.

We are witnessing today an amazing proliferation of pornography. It is almost impossible to go to a theater without encountering obscenity and foul talk. It is almost impossible to read a magazine (even a so-called "family" magazine) that does not feature articles and pictures on sex. We read of people who have become rich by turning their publishing or entertainment efforts toward filth and weakness.

We need to be realistic, of course. We can't ignore the facts that some humans are depraved and that life is sometimes brutal and unpleasant. But too many are becoming obsessed with the sensual side of life and have turned away from light and truth. I don't think God ever meant it to be that way. He has expressed hope that his children will use their minds for the improvement of man's existence, not the worsening of it.

There is something very rewarding about the pursuit of truth. There is an illumination of spirit that can only be attributed to the light of God. In every activity and phase of our existence, whether it be running a home or guiding a nation, we need to use our God-given intelligence. It is remarkable what great influence in the affairs of men the thoughts and ideas of a man of intelligence can give.

Man cannot bumble along nowadays like he used to do. In some areas of human affairs there is no room for error. In nearly all human enterprise there is no place for the ignorant and misinformed.

In my study, I have found a greater perception of the meaning of the word "glory," as used here in regard to intelligence. To me it signifies a heavenly exultation, the happiness of God.

It is good to know that the Lord glories in our intelligent pursuit. It is reassuring to know that we can turn to him for illumination and understanding. There is potent reason for inviting him to be with us in all of our affairs.

Humble

Therefore, blessed are they
who humble themselves
without being compelled
to be humble. . . .

—ALMA 32:16

The first question I asked myself at the beginning of the week of experiment upon this scripture was, Why humility? Why is it so important to be humble? And a corollary question: Why do we talk favorably about it? My answer to these questions may not satisfy everyone, but I quickly saw that people who are un-humble are generally arrogant, self-satisfied, and unteachable.

Along with this observation was my discovery that people who are humble are responsive and receptive. This difference led me to the answer that humility is necessary to learn. We are here on earth to learn, so we have to be open-minded (a part of being humble) to accept truth.

One wise person said that when you first say that you have humility is when you have just lost it. One does not boast of his humility. Nor can a person make a display of his alleged humility. If a person is to learn humility, he must do it quietly and sincerely.

Another observation is that the humble person

is not always the one who is withdrawn and shy. He is the one who wears his accomplishments lightly and realizes that no matter how well he succeeds he is still far from God's perfection—and perhaps even far from what he could be. He is oftentimes strong, but he knows that his earthly strength is of little consequence if he misuses it. He generally has ability and talent, but he knows that they are to be used in blessing mankind and not in acting selfishly.

When he prays to God, the humble one does not spend his time reminding the Lord of his good deeds; but — recognizing his failings — he talks with God about how he can be more useful in fulfilling the Lord's purposes. He sincerely has given priority to the Lord's plan and the well-being of mankind, rather than giving primary attention to his own interests.

Every man needs some reminders about humility. It is easy to become enraptured with one's own accomplishments and successes. One of the best ways to keep humble is to read often the first seven verses of Second Timothy, Chapter 3, for there it speaks of men becoming "lovers of their own selves. . . ."

I've asked myself: What are the qualities of humility? There is a very perceptive answer in Alma 7:23: ". . . submissive and gentle; easy to be entreated full of patience and long-suffering; being temperate . . .; being diligent . . . ; asking . . . ; always returning thanks unto God. . . ." These are virtues that I am seeking, and when I'm able to live by them perhaps I can be humble.

Healing

. . . he that hath faith in me
to be healed,
and is not appointed
unto death,
shall be healed.
He who hath faith to see shall see.
He who hath faith to hear shall hear.

—*D&C* 42:48-50

Faith healing is very much a part of the gospel of Jesus Christ. It is a great promise to those who wish to develop their spiritual resources. It is reassuring to know that God cares enough about the principle of healing that he would make this kind of commitment.

In order to be healed, of course, one must have faith.

The acquiring of faith requires a certain amount of wonderment, not credulity. This sense of wonderment led young Joseph Smith in 1820 to examine a scripture in the New Testament, James 1:5. The experience of reading this statement and then applying it led the young man to a new understanding of faith. His complete acceptance of God was built upon the "nothing wavering" idea cited in the sixth verse of James 1. It has helped me to know that "a double minded man is unstable in all his ways" (James 1:8).

Perhaps the best way to reach this frame of mind of complete confidence in God is to constantly school our mind and spirit.

Part of the marvelousness of the experience of being healed by faith is to feel its strength come into one's being. It is a kind of putting aside of physical pain in order to make way for the Spirit of God.

In a crisis, I've noted, one forgets about his bodily ailment. He is so absorbed in the current problem that for a few moments his ache or pain is forgotten. I conclude therefore that the act of faith is to give priority to heavenly power over bodily discomfort. It is the act of putting oneself into complete communion with the Lord. It is feeling that one is a part of divine influence and power so completely that the physical becomes absorbed in the spiritual.

Faith is also using one's mind to stay well and avoid illness. I think God is not pleased with the person who violates rules of good health. A person is closer to heaven if he honors the temple that God has given him. If he keeps it clean and shuns those things which would violate that temple, he lets the Lord know that he is appreciative of the blessing of life and health.

A wise person knows that good health is consistent with God's purposes. He knows that ill health is oftentimes a result of intemperance and violation of the Lord's commandments.

God is inviting us to both see and hear. Faith is the way.

Administer Relief

Think of your brethren
like unto yourselves. . . .
clothe the naked . . .
feed the hungry . . .
liberate the captive,
and administer relief
to the sick and afflicted.

—*JACOB 2:17, 19*

My thoughts have been turned to charity and regard for my fellowmen for two reasons: (1) we all need to think *outwardly* instead of selfishly, and (2) we are reaching a point in population growth and communications-closeness that we cannot wisely or safely ignore our fellowmen.

There are in our midst suffering people who need our help. We should always think of our fellowmen as we do ourselves, and at least a part of our time should be devoted to actually helping our needy brethren. The person who devotes all of his attention to himself is not only disobeying God but also passing up a precious opportunity to invest his humanity.

God has made it clear that "all flesh is mine, and I am no respecter of persons." (D&C 38:16.) We had better realize that we are no more loved of the Lord than our fellowmen.

There are almost limitless ways to serve. This scripture alludes to some but issues a general invitation to "administer relief" wherever necessary. We shouldn't assume that someone else will take care of the matter. We are not doing enough when we give a few dollars to a charity drive. Nor should we assume that our taxes, some of which are devoted to welfare, will do the job. So far mankind has never been able to overcome inequality and injustice, and I assume that there will always be those who need help. Only when all men give a helping hand to the weak and downtrodden will we get closer to a total alleviation of suffering. It's a desirable goal.

What we must overcome is identified in Mormon 8:37: ". . . ye do love money, and your substance, and your fine apparel . . . more than ye love the poor and needy, the sick and afflicted." Obviously, we need to change our value system. Our main goal in securing material things is to bless mankind by their use. We need to put our "love" in perspective.

Evil always comes when society begins "to be distinguished by ranks, according to their riches and their chances for learning. . . ." (3 Nephi 6:12.) When this happens, it is a sure sign that the admonitions to "think of your brethren like unto yourselves" has been forgotten or ignored by most of the people.

The time to start is now. Every good deed is an act of charity: you can open your eyes to life about you. You can encourage others. You can cheer up the sad. You can give guidance to the lost. You can remember the words of Mahomet: "A man's true wealth hereafter is the good he does in this world to his fellow man. When he dies, people will say, 'What property has he left behind him?' but the angels will ask, 'What good deeds has he sent before him?' "

Man

Man was also
in the beginning
with God. . . .

—D&C 93:29

In these eight words is a magnificent statement of man's identity. Man attains dignity as he understands that he is an eternal being with God. All aspects of human endeavor take on greater significance when one understands this principle, for man's work need not be perishable. If it is attuned to God's eternal purposes, it relates to a pre-earth life and has a permanence beyond the grave. These are insights that came to me during a week of intensive application of this scripture.

The cry of the individual is, "Someday I hope I can truly understand myself." It is the cry of self-identification. Every individual needs to know that he is important. When a person begins to understand that he is an entity and not just an immaterial part of a mass, he begins to appreciate his selfhood.

A recent news article told of a couple who had left a big city to live in relative isolation in a remote wilderness mountain cabin. The husband cited "a repulsion toward city life" as the reason for the drastic change, but the underlying idea that came through to me is that this couple too is searching for self-identity and a feeling of worth. I am certainly not opposed to reclusion, but I do believe that every person needs to be reminded of his importance.

There are many influences in the world that would remove or alter one's individuality. But we know that whenever we battle to preserve that individuality, we are working in the divine cause. We know that all efforts to "be myself" are in keeping with man's destiny.

It is exciting to consider that the personal word "man" is used rather than "men." This aspect of the scriptural statement stresses individuality. In a real sense, also, man has independence because he has an eternal selfhood. This does not imply independence *from* God, but independence *with* God.

Exhilaration of spirit, I believe, is with the God-man idea. We are—in the sense of this scripture——co-eternal with God. This concept, rather than lessening the importance of God, gives one the understanding that our Heavenly Father delights in our successes because of our special relationship with him. This statement does not change the fact that God is still in control and that he is omniscient.

I like the thoughts of E. G. Mesthene: "God and man are partners in the work of the world. . . ." The responsibility is on man, therefore, to have confidence in himself, to attain knowledge and skill, and to be potent in creating a better world. My feeling is that when man understands and accepts his divine nature, God will be grateful.

Plainness

. . . my soul delighteth
in plainness;
for after this manner
doth the Lord God work
among the children of men. . . .

—2 NEPHI 31:3

If every person would memorize the first two lines of this scripture and use it in all of his statements—both written and oral—there would not be so much confusion in the world.

People don't intend to be obscure or complex when they speak or write, but they end up being that way because they have not reminded themselves that plainness and simplicity are important in a fast-moving world. *Communication* is a popular word now, but the pamphlets and essays that extol the virtues of good communication generally fail to mention that plainness is the first ingredient of being understood by someone else.

This is the way the Lord speaks. This is the way he works "among the children of men." This is the way he would like us to be, both in communication with him and in all of our dealings with our fellowmen.

I invite you to try it for a few days. Whenever you prepare to describe something — even in conversation with a friend—think consciously about being plain. Think about being direct and simple and understandable. You'll be amazed that you are "connecting."

"But," you say, "my friends and those near to me understand me, as I understand them." Is it possible that your friends are pained by your verbosity? And what of all the others you meet and have dealings with? Do they understand you? Since memorizing this scriptural statement I have been especially sensitive to all that I read and hear. I recently saw a five-page plan for a series of conferences, and it never mentioned that there was a purpose for such meetings, nor was an indication given that there are goals to be accomplished.

I am reminded of John Ray's statement: "He that useth many words for the explaining of any subject, doth, like the cuttlefish, hide himself for the most part in his own ink."

The Lord has set the example. He is plain in his statements and stories. Jesus didn't try to embellish his parables or draw them out interminably. Whether you think about the wording of the Ten Commandments or the Sermon on the Mount, you can see the pattern of plainness that God has set.

A headline over a feature in a newspaper caught my eye: "Once, Long Ago, Simplicity Was the Keynote of Charm." My response is that it still should be. Great writing is simple and plain; wonderful people are uncomplicated and direct; and God is understandable and approachable.

Word

For you shall live
by every word
that proceedeth forth
from the mouth of God.

—*D&C* 84:44

God has said many things over the centuries for the benefit of man. A main purpose of this book is to begin to point out that there is probably nothing in man's "problem areas" that has not been touched on by our Father. It would be to our benefit, therefore, to become aware of what God has said and is saying. We can readily find it in the scripture ("by the mouth of all his holy prophets"), in direct communication with him, in meditation, and as we listen to inspired people.

My personal experience is based on the word "live" in this scripture. For 52 weeks I have actively tried to *live* by the Lord's revealed word. It has been an uplifting experience. I assure you that it is worth your attention.

Another phrase that attracts my concern is "by every word." It reminds me that it is not good for man to pick and choose among God's words. *All* that the Lord has said to man is good for man. It behooves me to try to learn all that God has spoken, even though it is a never-ending pursuit.

Most people, I have observed, have an idea that they would like to read the word of God. They have scriptural works in their home, but they rarely open them. Part of the problem seems to be that there may be too many other things to do. Another part of the problem is that people don't know how to read scripture. Once in a while they try, but they become discouraged because it doesn't read like a novel or even like a popular nonfiction work. I believe the key is to make scripture reading a habit: a little every day. A person can either allow a certain amount of time—say half an hour—or a certain number of pages every day. I have found that the latter method is better, and I suggest one or two chapters per day, which is not only "systematic," but —more important—lends itself to a more thoughtful consideration of scriptural messages.

I have found that when I read scripture I have a better experience when I try to encourage a spiritual mood, by seeking peace and quiet and erasing from my mind all outside thoughts. Then I can be more open-minded to God's message and sensitive to the possible enrichment of spirit.

Reading scripture, I assure you, is the foundation of learning about the words of God. When a person has embarked on this experience, he is preparing his mind and spirit to observe and listen in other ways. Chances are that he will become more aware of God's message as it may be found in the beauty of nature, in hearing the gospel message, in peaceful contemplation, in prayer.

This Moment

Improve the shining moments;
Don't let them pass you by . . .
And if we are not mindful,
The chance will fade away;
For life is quick in passing;
'Tis as a single day.

—*R. B. BAIRD, IN HYMNS, CHURCH OF JESUS CHRIST OF LATTER-DAY SAINTS, NO. 73*

Some questions about my way of living arose because of this hymnal message. Do I enjoy the present moment? Am I really aware? Do I really listen? Do I absorb and feel? Or do I live constantly in the future? Do I "lose the day in expectation of night, and night in fear of dawn"? (Seneca.) I decided that if I cannot enjoy the present, my life is troubled.

But the hymnologist is urging me to both enjoy and improve the shining moments. He is telling me that if I ignore it, "The chance will fade away."

When the world presses in upon me so that I begin to be fearful of life, it is wonderful to think that I can actually enjoy and improve *now*.

I have learned that I can improve the present by becoming aware of its significance: this exact situation will never be duplicated again (that is, "life is quick in passing"). Human relationships begin to mean more. Tomorrow—or "the next time"—may be too late. "The best things are nearest: breath in your nostrils, light in your eyes, flowers at your feet, duties at your hand, the path of Right just before you." (Robert Louis Stevenson.)

One philosopher-writer reminds me to be happy where I am and in what I'm doing, or I'll never be happy. There are students preparing for their careers who disagree with that. There are people who are ill who disagree. There are countless numbers who yearn for a better job or a better way of life who cannot, according to them, enjoy the present. I don't think we should be satisfied and apathetic about our present condition and cease striving—but we should enjoy life today, here, now.

Much in scripture confirms the message of this hymn. I'm assured that a loving Father in heaven is pleased when his children appreciate the sweetness and immediacy of life today. We never reach a point in life when time is no longer important to us. We can all—young or old—use our time to make life better and prepare to meet God.

A friend asked several of us if our lives have been a "blur." He said he had noticed that parts of his life had been that way whenever he "rushed through" existence and gave little time or attention to the present moment. The truth is, the future is unclear, and what is real is now. Rupert Brooke said that "our heaven is now."

I am grateful to the composer of this hymn, Mr. Baird, for putting forth a message that reminds me that these moments are precious, especially if I improve them.

Service

. . . when ye are in the service
of your fellow beings
ye are only in the service
of your God.

—MOSIAH 2:17

51 SERVICE

Some people think that one must withdraw from the world in order to be religious. Communication with God, it is generally thought, can only be had when one is alone.

But this scriptural statement (and several others) indicates to me that a person is in the Lord's service when he is working in the community. When a person can invest his humanity in helping the poor, the disadvantaged, the helpless, the oppressed, or the needy, he is serving God. When one sees the humane service of Dr. Albert Schweitzer in Africa, or Mahatma Gandhi's effective social and political service in India, one realizes how helping one's fellowmen is genuine worship of God.

However, we don't have to go to a far-off country to find humans in need. There are many opportunities close around us. In countless ways in every community there are those who need someone else: someone who cares and is willing to serve.

When one gives of himself ungrudgingly, he earns the praise of God. When he uses his talent, his intelligence, his knowledge to lift his fellowmen, his service is blessed on earth and in heaven.

There is a cry for "relevance" in the land; a cry that religion be related to the problems of the day and contribute its special moral sense to the improvement of the community. I'm sure that religion shouldn't forsake its sacred and spiritual role, nor become just another organization in local squabbles, but there is a real vacuum in community affairs if religious people are not actively engaged.

So take heart, you who love the church and who also love your community and feel that it needs your active interest. Know that the Lord is desirous of having you serve your fellow beings. That kind of dedicated service is strong evidence that you love God.

My practicing of this scripture caused me to take a new look at the idea of service: that it is greater than just doing one's duty. A young girl stated (rather plaintively), "I have friends; I want them to know that I love them; and I'd like to see them if they weren't so busy." Her comment made me think that to share oneself with others is a high type of service and is not considered in the realm of duty.

This is what is needed in our society—going about doing good. Participating in various programs of charity is fine, but people need people. They need to feel their warmth and humanity. We need to be a little less busy and more concerned about the needs of our fellowmen.

Experiment

. . . awake and arouse
your faculties,
even to an
experiment upon my words,
and exercise
a particle of faith. . . .

—*ALMA 32:27*

The word "experiment" comes from *experiri,* "to try," according to the dictionary. We try experiments on other things, so why not on spiritual things?

I know that God doesn't demand blind faith, but simply asks us just to experiment upon his words, i.e., to test the truth of what he says. If we will just "let this desire work," we can know for ourselves.

So, for all of us who falter, who lose faith, who do less than we are able and less than we should, the Lord invites us to simply "give place for a portion" of his words.

I am responding to this cordial, longing invitation. I would like you to know that I have the assurance that God loves me and that I am one of his children. As long as I live, I will know that he is inviting me to carefully examine his words.

People who profess to seek truth fall into one of three categories: (1) those who accept truth fully and probably without examination; (2) some who accept truth partially and with definite reservations; (3) a few who go to the "marrow of the bone" in a wholehearted, spiritually based search. The latter are the "experimenters." Their ultimate faith is sound because they are neither blind nor lukewarm. I hope to be in group three.

Based on my experience, I would like to suggest the following if you tend to be a skeptic, or if you find yourself being critical of religious people and religious belief: just say to yourself, "maybe it's true." Then give God a chance: ". . . exercise a particle of faith." Let him work in you. Look at the positive side of life: its beauty, its wholeness, its purpose. Look for the good in people—don't be engrossed with their failings.

Try prayer. Try to communicate with God. He'll listen to you. You may not know at first, because I believe he wants to know that you are really and seriously trying to experiment upon his words. When both you and he know that, a good feeling will come to you.

This scriptural statement from Alma is reminiscent of a similar bit of advice from John 7:17: "If any man will do his will, he shall know of the doctrine, whether it be of God, or whether I speak of myself."

I conclude this series of scriptural statements and essays by saying that these scriptures are "of God." In applying them to one's life—in experimenting with them—there is joy and a wonderful sense of fulfillment.

Index